George Stuart Fullerton

On Sameness and Identity

A Psychological Study

George Stuart Fullerton

On Sameness and Identity
A Psychological Study

ISBN/EAN: 9783743369252

Manufactured in Europe, USA, Canada, Australia, Japa

Cover: Foto ©Thomas Meinert / pixelio.de

Manufactured and distributed by brebook publishing software (www.brebook.com)

George Stuart Fullerton

On Sameness and Identity

Publications of the University of Pennsylvania

PHILOSOPHICAL SERIES.

EDITED BY

GEORGE STUART FULLERTON
Professor of Philosophy
AND
JAMES McKEEN CATTELL
Professor of Psychology.

ON SAMENESS AND IDENTITY.

A PSYCHOLOGICAL STUDY: BEING A CONTRIBUTION TO THE FOUNDATIONS
OF A THEORY OF KNOWLEDGE.

BY

GEORGE STUART FULLERTON.

On Sameness and Identity.

PART I.

THE KINDS OF SAMENESS.

And some require everything accurately stated; whereas, this accuracy annoys others,
either because of their inability to follow a train of reasoning through, or because of its hair-
splitting character; for accuracy does involve some hair-splitting.

Aristotle, Metaph. Book I, The Less, c. 3.

SECTION I. There are few words the ambiguity of which has
led to more confusion and profitless dispute than that of the word
same. Men constantly use this word as though it had but one
meaning, and that meaning were always clear, whereas it really
gives expression to a number of widely different experiences,
some of which are quite difficult of analysis. It is highly desira-
ble that these experiences should not be confounded with each
other, but kept clearly separate, as the consequences of such
misconception are very far-reaching. How far-reaching, I shall
in the pages to follow try to indicate.

It is my purpose to point out the differences in connotation of
the several senses of this highly ambiguous word, to show the
element which they have in common, and to trace some of the
difficulties and absurdities which have sprung from using the
word loosely and without proper discrimination. I shall have to
plead guilty to something very like hair-splitting, but I may put
forward in excuse the undeniable fact that "accuracy does
involve some hair-splitting." If anyone prefers the self-contra-
dictions and preposterous conclusions to which loose and unana-
lytic thought has so often led the unwary, he is welcome to them.
I shall hold a few of these up to inspection after a while. For
my part, I prefer a little quibbling at the outset of a discussion

to a systematic incoherence all through it, with the chances of finding myself in a *cul-de-sac* at the end. Whether I am successful in dissipating to some degree the fog which has hung about samenesses and obliterated important distinctions, each one must judge for himself.

The kinds of sameness I find to be as follows :

SEC. 2. I. We speak of any sensation, feeling, or idea, or complex of sensations, feelings, or ideas, as being the same with itself at any one instant. The pain in my finger is what it is at this moment. The finger itself (the immediate object of knowledge, a complex from sense and imagination) is, at each moment, what it is. It is to this sense of the word that the logical laws of Identity and Contradiction have ultimate reference.

SEC. 3. II. A sensation, feeling, or idea, or complex of sensations, feelings, or ideas, considered in itself and without reference to the world of material things, is called the same with one previously existent when the two are alike. I say, for example, that I feel to-day the same pain I felt yesterday, or that I have dreamt the same dream three times. This is evidently not sameness of the kind first mentioned.

SEC. 4. III. We speak of seeing the same material thing at different times. Suppose a man passing along a country road to look across a field at a distant tree. What he actually sees is a small bluish patch of color, which, interpreting in terms furnished by his previous experience, he supplements with material drawn from memory and imagination. On the following day he looks at the tree again from a nearer point and sees a larger green patch of color with distinct differences of shading and with a clear outline. This he interprets in a similar manner.

Now, without being a philosopher at all, and without conscious reference to anything beyond what he has experienced or can experience, he affirms that he has on two successive days seen the same tree. I ask, just what is the significance of the word same as used in this connection? What peculiar experience has it been employed to mark? What is perceived on the one occa sion is not the same as what is perceived on the other in the sense of the word first given (by "perceived" I mean existing in consciousness as a complex of mental elements. With the sup posed external correlates of our percepts I am not now con cerned). And it is equally clear that two such percepts need not be the same in the second sense of the word, for they may be quite unlike. In this case they are unlike, so far at least as what is actually in sensation is concerned.

What peculiar experience then does the word mark when the observer declares that he has seen the same tree twice?

We are now in the sphere of material objects (*i. e.*, as experi enced; I refer to the mental content and nothing more), and are not concerned with our experiences as isolated elements, but as grouped and arranged in series. Our total possible experience of any one object is a collection of partly simultaneous and partly successive actual and possible sensations which condi tion each other, and which we regard as a unit. The Idealist believes that this is all there is of the object, and all we mean when we commonly employ the word. The Realist assumes that there is something beyond and corresponding to this expe rience, and which is to be regarded as the real thing. He, how ever, must admit that all we can know of any object, in what ever sense we choose to employ that word, all our evidence for maintaining its existence and determining its qualities, must be drawn from this group of sensations. It is this that we immedi ately know, and anything inferred must be inferred from this.

From this it follows that when any one, whether Realist, or Idealist, or unreflective man, feels justified in asserting that what he perceives to-day is the same object he perceived yesterday, he is led to make this assertion on the strength of some distinction in his immediate experience, and he refers only secondarily, if at all, to anything beyond and external to this. The distinction which he marks by the word is this : He has reason to believe that the two percepts in question belong to the one series,—to the one life history, so to speak. He believes that had he cared to do so he could have filled up the gap between them by a continuous series of percepts, each conditioned by the preceding, and forming the one chain. Each represents to him the one object, in that each stands for the whole series, and his thought is much more taken up with the series as a whole than with the individuals composing it. He knows that the percepts in such a series can only be successive, never simultaneous. Had he reason to suspect that the two percepts we are discussing belong to different series of this kind, and that there is nothing in the nature of the case to prevent their being simultaneous, he would decide for two trees.

But each percept contains more than one mental element, and just as we may regard each percept as representing the whole series, so we may regard each element as representing the whole complex which may be experienced at one time, and through this the whole series of percepts. I say that the orange I smell is the same with the one I see ; that I can reveal by striking a light the chair I fell over in the dark ; that I hear rattling down the street the coach I stepped out of a few moments ago. It is not worth while to distinguish this use from the use of the word same just mentioned, for they agree in making a single experience stand for a whole group or series, which is assumed to be at least potentially present with each one. When we have had two experiences thus representing the one group, we say that we have in two ways, or on two occasions, experienced the same object. In this sense has the man in our illustration seen yesterday and to-day the same tree. In this sense could he at the one time see and touch the same tree.

It is in this sense also that we use the word when we say that the object seen with the naked eye and the object seen through a telescope or under a microscope are the same. If I look at a distant object with the naked eye and then look at it through a telescope, what I actually see (or what is actually in the sense) is in the two cases very different. But just as seeing an object from a distance with the naked eye, I may walk towards it and substitute for the dim and vague percept which I first had a series of percepts increasing in clearness and ending in one which I regard as altogether satisfactory, so I may substitute at once this clear percept for the dim one, by the use of the telescope, and may know that it properly belongs to the series which, taken as a whole, constitutes my notion of the object. This I may know from the relations which this percept bears to the other percepts of the series, and which allow me to pass in my inferences from it to them as I can from any one of them to another. If, seeing a dim object upon the horizon, I raise a telescope and through it perceive the figure of a man, I know that I could have had a similar percept without any telescope by simply approaching the object. Conversely, on perceiving a man near at hand, I know I could have a similar percept from a distance by looking through a telescope. I call the man seen through the telescope the same as the man seen with the naked eye, for the same reason as I call the man seen by the eye at a distance the same with the man seen near at hand.

And the apparently non-extended speck which I see with the naked eye looks very different from the curious insect I see when I place a microscope over this speck, but I call them the same for the reason just given. If the insect as seen under the glass be divided, so is the speck as seen by the eye; if the insect is taken away, the speck disappears too. The series of percepts made possible through the microscope may be regarded as a continuation of the series which arises from approaching the eye to the object. Each member in it stands in a relation to this primary series similar to that illustrated above in the case of the telescope, and similar to that held by the terms of the primary series to each other. It should be kept clearly in mind that in all these cases the object (immediately perceived) is the same only in the sense pointed out, *i. e.*, two or more percepts, which may, in themselves considered, be quite unlike each other, are recognized as in a certain relation to each other, as each representing the one series to which all belong. If one thinks he has reason to believe each percept represents not merely the series of percepts, but something different, which he infers and is pleased to call the "real" thing, he may be inclined to believe that in saying he sees the same object on two occasions he is referring to this something. It must be clear to him, however that all his evidence for the sameness of this something lies in the experience I have described, and it is to this that he must point in proof that it is the same. The percepts themselves are certainly not the same in any other sense than the one given. They are not identical, and they need not be alike. They merely stand for each other. Should one forget this, he will fall into blunders which I will illustrate at length when I speak of the common opinion on the subject of the infinite divisibility of space.

John Locke, in his famous "Essay,"[1] has made a distinction between the sameness of masses of inorganic matter and the sameness of organisms. That of the former, he says, consists in the sameness of their particles, while the sameness of a plant or animal does not consist in that of the particles which com-

---

[1] Essay Concerning Human Understanding, Bk. 2, Chap. 27, § 3.

pose it at this time or at that, for they are in continual flux, but in the participation in the one life of the organism. It does not, however, appear to me that we have here a real difference in the kind of experience marked by the word. The difference is merely that in the one case we connect this experience, not with the object as a whole, but with the separate particles which compose it, which we take as so many separate objects each having a sameness of the kind just discussed, while in the other case we look upon the object as a whole, as a unit, and disregard any reference to its component parts. But whether we regard the object as a unit or take each of its ultimate parts as separate objects, we are thinking of the one kind of sameness. We are thinking of a certain life-history in which any one link may represent the whole, and any two links may be, from this point of view, regarded as equivalent. It is not merely with reference to plants and animals that we speak of sameness without regard to a sameness of constituent parts. We do it in this case simply because the organism furnishes us with a convenient unit, and one much more important as a unit than as an aggregate. We can make similar units when we please, and consider their sameness without thinking of their parts. We speak of the same nation as existing through many generations, and of the same corporation as surviving many deaths. Whether the object we are considering be naturally indivisible, or composite and assumed a unit for convenience, when we speak of it as the same at two different times we are referring to the one experience. Locke does make here a distinction worth noticing, but it does not mark two fundamentally different uses of the word.

Sec. 5. IV. Two objects are called the same, and two other mental experiences occurring at the one time are called the same, from the fact that they are recognized as alike. The botanist, finding that two plants belong to the one class calls them the same without any intention of confounding the two individuals. Nor does one who places his two hands in warm water and declares that he has the same feeling in both, confound the two streams of sensation. The fact that only likeness is meant is here clearly recognized. It is not, I think, as clearly recognized when similar sensations or other mental experiences (considered singly), occurring at *different* times, are called the same. In that case they are sometimes spoken of as if they were material objects having a continuous sameness after the fashion explained above.

Sec. 6. V. The word same is used to signify the relation between any mental experience and that which is regarded as its representative. This representative may or may not resemble it. We speak, for example, of calling up in memory this or that object seen at some past time. The memory-image is certainly not the same with the original percept in Sense I. When we say that the object of memory is the past, we cannot mean this, for it is plainly false. Nor is it thought of as merely like it, as in Sense II. It is thought of as a something which represents it—stands for it in a peculiar way. Just what this implies I will not here attempt to discover. It is enough for my purpose to point out that when we say a man remembers an object we do not mean merely to indicate the presence in his imagination of a resembling picture, but to include a certain relation between this picture and an original percept.

It is not easy to describe what is present in an act of memory. When I am thinking of another man as calling to mind something from his past experience, I bring before my own mind two pictures, one representing his original percept, and one his present memory-image. Holding these before me together, I recognize them as related, but distinct. I use the word same to denote their relation. But the person who is exercising his memory does not have before his mind two objects, an original and a copy, with an observed relation between them. He has not the original, or it would not be an act of memory. When, however, he reflects upon his experience as I have done, he represents it to himself as I have represented it to myself. He speaks as if, in the act of remembering, he were conscious of two objects and could compare them. He speaks of recognizing the memory picture as a copy and representative of the original percept. Language, as commonly used, adapts itself to this way of regarding the matter, and I may leave a further analysis of it to the student of the memory, merely pointing out that, whatever is implied in the experience, a common use of the word same is to denote this relation between any mental experience and the memory-image which represents it.

It will be seen that this kind of sameness may be presupposed in affirming sameness in other senses of the word. When I compare a present sensation with one felt some days since, and affirm that they are the same, the latter must enter into the comparison through its representative in memory. It is not itself present at the time of the comparison.

And when I say that I have seen the same tree yesterday and to-day, I mean, as I have explained, that the two percepts belong to the one series; but since my experience of yesterday cannot be itself present in my consciousness to-day, it can take its place in the series, as thought to-day, only by proxy. When I say that I have in my mind the same series on two successive days, I evidently mean that it is the same series in the sense in which any experience and its representative in memory are the same.

Other less important instances might be given of this use of the word same to express the relation between any experience and its representative. We say that we see an object in a mirror, when we mean that we see its reflected image. We speak of seeing in a picture this man or that. When we have found for anything a satisfactory substitute we say it is the same thing. Such uses of the word are not likely to deceive anyone, and I will not dwell upon them. Their meaning is too plain to be mistaken.

SEC. 7. VI. We constantly speak of two men as seeing the same thing. In this we have a sense of the word which demands careful analysis. For the sake of clearness, and to avoid ambiguity, I will confine myself here, as I have done in the foregoing sections, to an examination of what is actually experienced by the men, and will defer all consideration of existences assumed as lying beyond a possible experience in an extramental world, for discussion in sections to follow.

The question which interests me at present is simply this: What experience is it that leads a man to affirm that he and someone else are perceiving the same object? The Realist (in the modern sense) would say that this experience is only his evidence that he and another are perceiving the same object, meaning by object what I have referred to as believed to lie beyond his experience; while the Idealist would say that this experience exhausts the whole matter. The Realist must, however, admit, as I have brought out in a different connection, that all his evidence for the existence of the object (in his sense), and for any affirmations whatever regarding it, lying within the field of the immediately known, any words, which have been coined to express qualities of, or distinctions concerning, this object, would retain a use and significance as marking distinctions within this field even if the object were supposed nonexistent. Whether any such duplicate of what is immediately perceived exists or not is a question apart. Since we admittedly draw all our distinctions from the field of the immediately known and then carry them over to such objects, and not *vice versa*, we may be sure that we would go on saying that two men see the same object in any case. I myself give the preference to that the existence of which is an indubitable fact, and prefer using the word *object* to indicate the complex in consciousness. I have, however, no desire to assume any point in dispute by juggling with a word, and will try to keep clearly in mind the meaning of the word thus assumed whenever I use it.

Now, the experience which leads me to say that I and another man see the same object is just this : I perceive a particular object, and in a certain relation to it I perceive the body of another man. From a past experience of my own body in relation to objects and from reasoning by analogy, I have come to connect such a relation of another body to the object with the thought of another consciousness of the object as connected with that body. Just as I perceive my own body to perform certain actions when I am conscious of perceiving the object, so I perceive this other body with which I have connected in thought a consciousness of the object to perform similar acts in response to similar relations towards the object. It is wholly a matter of observation in my own case that the perception of my own body in this or that relation to an object is a *sine qua non* to the perception of the object. And it is wholly a matter of reasoning from like to like that leads me to connect in thought sensations or percepts with any other animal body whatever. When I say, therefore, that I and another man are perceiving the same thing, there is in my mind a complex consisting of a percept or idea of the thing, a percept or idea of the man's body, and the thought of a percept connected with this body. When I say that he is thinking of us both as seeing the same thing, I call up in mind a similar complex and connect it in thought with his body. Whatever I may believe as to the existence or non-existence of things lying beyond this sphere, and supposed to cause these experiences, these are the experiences to which I ultimately refer when I speak of two men as seeing the same object, and these furnish the whole ground for the existence of the phrase.

The percept of the object which I connect in thought with the other man's body need not be wholly similar to my percept of the object. The man who has discovered that he is color-blind, does not suppose that men not similarly afflicted see just what he does in looking at a cherry tree full of ripe fruit. Nevertheless, he still speaks of himself and others as seeing the same objects. If another man's body is not exactly like mine, I am not justified by argument from similarity in reading into it an exactly similar experience. It is not the similarity of the two percepts that I am thinking of chiefly when I speak of them as percepts of the same object. I am thinking of the relation in which I suppose them to stand to each other. I think of the possible existence of the one under given circumstances as conditioning the possible existence of the other.

Sec. 8. VII. When a man in an early stage of reflection upon his experience has decided that objects immediately perceived are not the real things but merely their mental copies or representatives, he may think of these "real" things in several ways. He may believe in a world of "real" things, consisting of groups of "real" qualities, external to consciousness; he may accept such "real" things, but add to them a substratum or substance, distinct from the qualities; or he may believe that the "real" exists as mere substratum, substance, or noumenon, and that all qualities, being merely its revelation to mind, exist within the circle of consciousness alone. The first position is one not often taken. The second is that held by Locke,[1] who believed

---

[1] Essay Concerning Human Understanding. Bk. 2, Chap. 2, § 1, and Bk. 2, Chap. 23, § 1. *et seq.*

that, corresponding to our ideas of objects, there exist substances possessed of certain primary qualities, and having an underlying substance or substratum. The third represents the view of the Kantian,[1] who, to be consistent, must deny to his noumenon any qualities whatever. How he is to do this without having it lapse into utter nothingness is a problem for him to solve.

The disciple of Locke has, therefore, in discussing all the uses of the word same, to consider the sameness of:

1. Things immediately known.

2. Groups of "real" qualities in an extra-mental world, more or less like what is immediately known.

3. Substance; the "I know not what" to which Locke clung through all difficulties.

The man who holds the first of the three views above mentioned need only consider the first and the second of these; and the Kantian need only consider the first and the third, rebaptizing the latter "noumenon" or "thing-in-itself."

Omitting for later consideration the sameness of the self or ego, I have already discussed the uses of the word same within the field of the immediately known. It remains to consider the sameness of what is believed to lie beyond this, and to belong to a different kind of a world.

When men discuss these supposed realities, in what senses of the word same may they reasonably think of them as the same?

---

[1] Kritik der reinen Vernunft.—"Von dem Grunde der Unterscheidung aller Gergenstände überhaupt in *Phænomena* und *Noumena*." Kant's Sämmtliche Werke, herausgegeben von Hartenstein. Leipzig, 1867, 3er Band, s. 209, *et seq.* See also, Kritik der Praktischen Vernunft; Vorrede; and the discussion: "Wie eine Erweiterung der reinen Vernunft in praktischer Absicht, ohne damit ihr Erkenntniss als speculativ, zugleich zu erweitern, zu denken möglich sei?" I Th. II B. II Hptst.; same edition, 5er Bd., s. 5, 140. I am not concerned here with the inner contradiction of the Kantian system. The notion of noumena predominantly in Kant's mind, was, I think, about as I have stated. He would not, of course, have denied "reality" to phenomena, but his misconception of Berkeley, and the satisfaction with which he settles down to the noumenal in the Critique of the Practical Reason, show that he felt toward the "blos Erscheinung" very much as Locke felt toward mere ideas. Cf. "Essay," Bk. 4, Chap. 11, § 7.

When a common, unreflective man, whose mind has not been, in the words of Bishop Berkeley, "debauched by learning," looks at a tree and thinks about it, he believes he sees a real tree, at a certain real distance from his body, and of a given real height and figure. It does not occur to him to make any distinction between the tree immediately perceived, and an inferred second tree, not immediately perceived, but represented by the former. There is the tree; he sees it; he can touch it ; it seems to him but one: and he always talks as if there were but one tree to be discussed in the premises. That one tree, he thinks, is really extended; is really out in space beyond his body; is, in short, what it appears to be. To his unreflective mind this tree does not seem to be a representative or to be seen through a representative, but to be seen immediately and just where it really is.

But when a man has begun to battle with the difficulties of reflection, and has learned to make a distinction between things and his ideas of the things, he will probably fall into unforeseen perplexities about this tree. He reflects that, when he closes his eyes, the tree disappears; that when he approaches it it looks green, and when he recedes from it it grows blue; that a man with a peculiar defect in his vision does not see it colored as he does; that when he makes a pressure on the side of one eyeball he sees two trees where before he saw only one; that when he makes such a pressure upon both eyeballs and moves them about a little he sees two trees moving about, although he knows real trees can not ordinarily be made to move about so easily. Such reflections lead him to distinguish between the tree as he sees it, and the tree as it really is, and he defines the tree as he sees it as the tree immediately known, and the real tree as the tree mediately known, a cause of the existence of the former. He now thinks that he sees directly only copies or representatives of real things, and as he believes these copies or representatives to be in his mind, and usually talks as if his mind were in his head, or at least in his body, he concludes that things immediately known must in many instances be much smaller than they seem, or perhaps lack extension altogether. How can a tree thirty feet high be in a man's mind? It is true, that, when I press upon my eyeballs in the manner described, I seem to see two trees of that size moving; but must it not be a mistake? Must we not assume that what is immediately seen only *seems* extended, and stands for an extended thing which is grasped through it? So our philosopher learns to distrust the immediate object of knowledge; to regard it as in some sense unreal as compared with what it represents; and to deny to it those properties which it apparently possesses. It is not extended, but it stands for extension; it is not colored, but it stands for color; it is not real, but it stands for reality.

It is natural, however, for one who has gone thus far to go farther. When he reflects again upon the fact that he sees the tree of a different color at different distances; when he remembers that colors vary with the quality of the light by which they are seen; when he and his neighbor dispute concerning the true color of the one tree which he sees dotted with red leaves, and which his opponent claims to see of a uniform color; then he may well begin to ask himself what is the true color of the "real" tree, or whether it is certain that it has any color at all? May not, then, the "real" tree have only some of the qualities that we ordinarily attribute to trees? Perhaps, the space qualities?

Or, worse yet, since some of the qualities that the ordinary man attributes to trees may be regarded as existing only in a shadowy way in our ideas, why may not the same be true of all the other qualities? How do we know that "real" trees are extended? How do we know that "real" extension must be assumed as the cause of the delusive apparent extension of our ideas, if it is true that "real" color need not thus be assumed as a cause of our sensations of color? What if the "real" thing exists only as an indescribable and incomprehensible somewhat, which we must assume as a cause of the immediately known, but of which we can know nothing more? When one has once begun this slippery descent, it is not easy to say where he may find a peg to stay him in his course.

Suppose, however, he is content to strip the "real" thing of what are commonly called the secondary qualities of matter, and to leave to it what are known as the primary. He will follow the example of the wholly unreflective man and speak of it in such a way as to suggest that the thing itself is something apart from its "real" qualities. A tree, he will say, *has* qualities. It would certainly sound odd to hear him say it *is* qualities. And he will very possibly go on to justify the use of the language he employs by distinguishing between the "real" qualities represented by his mental picture of the tree and an obscure something which he assumes as underlying them; thus embracing the Lockian distinction of ideas, "real" qualities, and substance. He may conclude, it is true, that substance in this sense of the word is chimerical, and that the belief in it arises out of a misunderstanding of the significance of language; but if he has gone so far as to assume duplicates of things immediately known, in the form of "real" qualities, it is more probable that he will be inclined to complete his classes of beings by adding the third.[1]

Now, it does not concern me to consider whether this change of view is to be regarded as a real progress in reflective knowledge or as a progressive decline and fall of the unreflective man.

---

[1] There is, of course, no reason why he may not add as many more classes as he pleases, and justify the additions as he justifies this. Men do not do this, as a matter of fact, but that is no reason.

The point which concerns me is this : The unreflective man talks as if but one tree were under discussion. The man who reflects uses the same forms of speech: and even when he believes that he must distinguish between the tree immediately known and the obscure something which he has come to look upon as its cause, or between the tree immediately known, the bundle of "real" qualities inferred, and the obscure something that he connects with these, he still goes on talking as if he had only one thing to talk about. The danger of such a proceeding is obvious. If I talk about two or three things as though they were one, it is but natural that I should sometimes confuse them with each other. Should proof be forthcoming for one of these, it would be but natural for me to fall occasionally into the error of supposing that it somehow applies to the others. If I go on saying "the tree" when I mean one tree and something else, two trees, or two trees and something else, it is only to be expected that I sooner or later come to grief in my reasonings.

And it should be noted that this peculiar ambiguity in the names of things entails a parallel ambiguity in the use of the words by which we indicate the mind's recognition of the presence of things. We commonly speak of a drunken man's *seeing* two trees, where a sober man sees one. We speak of an insane man as *hearing* voices, when no one has spoken. We say that we *see* the maples are turning red, even when we believe that color may not properly be attributed to the mediate object of knowledge. On the other hand, those who hold to the existence of "real" objects of the kind before mentioned, generally maintain that in referring to things in space, their positions and mutual relations, we are giving attention, not to the immediately known, but to its "external" double. " I see, feel, perceive," it is "said, not the image, and not the constituents of the image (the ideas), but the external object by *means* of the image."[1]

[1] Ueberweg. See Krauth's Ed. of Berkeley's "Principles," Phila., 1874, p. 343.

If one holds that this "external" object presupposes a substance, a something distinct from a group of qualities, there is nothing to prevent his maintaining, should he wish to do so, that in saying "I see a tree," primary reference is had to this substance or "reality." Of course, if, in the sentence "I see a tree," the word "tree" can have three meanings, it follows that there is also a possibility of taking in three senses the word "see." It is hardly necessary to point out that, unless one is very careful, "seeing" in one sense may result in "believing" in another, as "kicking" did in the famous case of Dr. Johnson and the stone. The caution is pertinent with respect to any other word used in the same general way as we use the word "see."

I have said that when a man abandons his original unreflective position and learns to distinguish between things immediately known and other things they are supposed to represent, he goes on using the common language, and talking as though there were but one thing under consideration. Now, men do not do this merely in common conversation and in writing about matters of everyday life, but they do it in the very books that have been written to prove that each thing is thus double or triple. John Locke, for example, begins the very chapter in which he is about to draw the distinction between the secondary and primary qualities of bodies (*i. e.*, between the constituents of things immediately known and the constituents of their "external" correlates), as well as to enlighten us on our ideas of substances, with the following words:[1]

"The mind being, as I have declared, furnished with a great number of the simple ideas, conveyed in by the senses, as they are found in exterior things, or by reflexion on its own operations, takes notice also, that a certain number of these simple ideas go constantly together; which, being presumed to belong

"Essay" Bk. 2, Chap. 23, § 1.

to one thing, and words being suited to common apprehensions, and made use of for quick despatch, are called, so united in one subject, by one name ; which, by inadvertency, we are apt afterward to talk of, and consider as one simple idea, which indeed is a complication of many ideas together : because, as I have said, not imagining how these simple ideas can subsist by themselves, we accustom ourselves to suppose some *substratum* wherein they do subsist, and from which they do result, and which therefore we call *substance*."

It is clear enough from this, as it is clear enough from other passages in the same book, that Locke talked as though the complex of simple ideas in consciousness were the very same thing (in Sense I) as the group of "real" qualities outside of consciousness. And no careful reader of his book can avoid seeing that the confusion of his language is a fair index to the confusion of his thoughts with regard to the two.[1] It is little better in the case of "bodies" and substance. In the passage just given, he would seem to make *substance* an obscure something underlying groups of ideas, and not groups of real qualities, but in the next sentence he makes it a substratum of the qualities which produce in us ideas. In many passages[2] he distinguishes between *substance* and *substances*, by which latter he means groups of "real" qualities with the added substratum or substance ; as such substances he instances oak, elephant, iron. He emphasizes the fact that substance is not to be confounded with substances, which are things of different sorts.[3] In so far as the substances are bundles of qualities, they are known to us through sensation.[4] In so far as they are also substance, they cannot be known to us through sensation, for the idea of substance is not known

---

[1] "Essay," Bk. 4, Chap. 2, § 14 ; Bk. 4, Chap. 4 and Chap. 11.

[2] *Ibid.*, Bk. 2, Chap. 12, § 6 ; Bk. 2, Chap. 23, § 1, with note (Phila., 1846, p. 183, *et seq.*).

[3] See note to § 1, Chap. 23, Bk. 2.   [4] Bk. 4, Chap. 11, *et passim*.

through sensation.[1] We are not then to look upon substance as such a constituent part of "a substance" as a quality is. The two belong to different classes. And if we offer proof for the existence of "real" substances, which is evidently applicable to them only as bundles of qualities—proof from sensation—then substance is overlooked altogether. It is significant that Locke, having thus put together under one head as "a substance" an oak viewed as a bundle of "real" qualities and an oak viewed as substratum, proceeded to argue as if he had but one thing to prove when he felt called upon to defend the real existence of substances. In his chapters on "The Extent of Human Knowledge," the "Reality of Knowledge," and "Our Knowledge of the Existence of Other Things,"[2] he devotes himself wholly to proving things as bundles of qualities, and pays no more attention to substance than if it had never entered his thought. If we take these chapters as authoritative, we must banish substance from the sphere of knowledge altogether.

As another instance of a use of language calculated to produce confusion, I may offer the following from Sir William Hamilton: "Whatever we know is not known as it is, but only as it seems to us to be,"[3]—a use of words which would certainly indicate that the immediate and mediate objects of knowledge are one. And what would we infer from such a sentence as this: "Thus the consciousness of an Inscrutable Power manifested to us through all phenomena, has been growing ever clearer; and must eventually be freed from its imperfections. The certainty that on the one hand such a Power exists, while on the other hand its nature transcends intuition and is beyond imagination, is the certainty towards which intelligence has from the first been progress-

---

[1] "I confess there is another idea, which would be of general use for mankind to have, as it is of general talk, as if they had it ; and that is the idea of substance, which we neither have, nor can have, by sensation or reflection." Bk. 1, Chap. 4, § 18 of the "Essay."

[2] "Essay," Bk. 4, Chaps. 3, 4 and 11.

[3] Lectures on Metaph., VIII, N. Y., 1880, p. 102.

ing."[1]   Or this: "We are obliged to regard every phenomenon
as a manifestation of some Power by which we are acted upon;
though Omnipresence is unthinkable, yet, as experience dis-
closes no bounds to the diffusion of phenomena, we are unable
to think of limits to the presence of this Power; while the criticisms of Science teach us that this Power is Incomprehensible.
And this consciousness of an Incomprehensible Power, called Om-
nipresent from inability to assign its limits, is just that consciousness on which Religion dwells."[2]

"After concluding that we cannot know the ultimate nature
of that which is manifested to us, there arise the questions—
What is it that we know?   In what sense do we know it?"[3]   Or
what shall one say to this: "Our consciousness of the unconditioned being literally the unconditioned consciousness, or raw
material of thought, to which in thinking we give definite forms,
it follows that an ever-present sense of real existence is the very
basis of our intelligence."[4]

Now, if the consciousness of an "inscrutable power" is not the
"inscrutable power" itself; if the existence of such a "power"
does not mean simply its existence in consciousness; if the
phenomena in which, it is assumed, a "power" is manifested,
are to be kept separate in thought from the "power," so that we
shall be in no danger of confounding a consciousness of certain
phenomena with consciousness of an "incomprehensible power;"
if our "consciousness of the unconditioned" is to be kept in mind
as signifying merely our "unconditioned consciousness," and an
"ever-present sense of real existence" as signifying only an
ever-present sense of "raw material" in consciousness; then it is
high time that these sentences and all such as these be re-written

[1] Herbert Spencer, "First Principles." Part I, Chap. V, § 31, N. 1, 1555, p. 168.
[2] "First Principles." Part I, Chap. V, § 27.
[3] Part II, Chap. I, § 35.   [4] Part I, Chap. IV, § 26.

with some regard for lucidity, accuracy and consistency. How can a reader help confounding things when he is thus taught by the very man whose business it is to distinguish between them? The blind led by the blind is a cheerful spectacle compared with this.

Nothing can be more evident than that the man who has abandoned his original unreflective belief in the singleness of the perceived object, and has come to believe in it as having one or more "external" correlates, should keep distinctly in mind that an immediate and a mediate object are, by hypothesis, two distinct things: that he has never had any direct experience whatever save of the one; and that all distinctions that he makes with regard to the other, the very notions of its existence, reality, and externality, have been drawn from the sphere of the immediate and carried over to it in thought. And he should never allow himself to forget, that, when he says he has passed in thought from the immediate to the mediate object, he cannot mean literrally that his thought is now occupied directly upon this "external" thing—that it is itself present to mind. He should remember that he can only mean that he has such an experience as the following:

He has in mind the immediate object, and a mental picture of a duplicate of this standing in a causal relation to it and represented by it; or, he has (if a Lockian), in addition to these two, a third highly vague and indefinite mental image (the idea of "substance"), which he connects with the image just described, as he has connected that with the immediate object; or (if a Kantian), he has in mind the immediate object, and, connected directly with that, such a vague image as has just been described. This is what he actually has in mind so far as *objects* are concerned. He does not, however, merely recognize the existence in his mind of these different images in their relations to each other, but he looks upon this mental arrangement as somehow justified by experience and embodying truth.

When we ask what the word *"justified"* can mean in this connection, it is not easy to find an answer. Within the sphere of the immediately known the meaning of the word is plain enough. When I have constructed in my imagination a certain image or complex of images embodying a belief as to matter of fact, I say the mental operation is justified when I can substitute for the idea the percept which it is supposed to represent, or can know indirectly that this might be done according to known laws of the appearance and disappearance of percepts. Thus I perceive the outside of a tree-trunk and form an idea of what lies under the bark. I have reason to know that by stripping off the bark I can substitute for the image I have formed the corresponding percept. And if I see at a distance a similar tree growing upon an inaccessible cliff, and form an image of what lies under its bark, I may still regard this as justified by the possibility of referring to cases in which a similar image, arising out of a similar experience, has been found to be justified. It is a legitimate inference that, if circumstances were somewhat different, the proper percept might take the place of this image too. It is evident, however, that the word "justified" cannot be used in this or any analogous sense in speaking of the relation not of an image to a percept, but of an image or a percept to a something that, by hypothesis, cannot itself enter into experience at all. What then can the word mean? It at first interests us to know that "some Snarks are Boojums," but our interest lapses when we discover that we have absolutely no mark by which we may know a Boojum from anything else.

But I must not be drawn into digressions. The points with which I am concerned are these:—FIRST: When a man says he sees this tree or that house, he ordinarily speaks as if there were but the one object in his thought. If he distinguishes at all between an immediate and a mediate object, the language that he uses would not indicate that he does so. And even after men have entered into lengthy arguments for the purpose of marking this distinction, and insisting that things are not single as they seem to the unreflective, they still indulge in this peculiar use of language, which would imply either that they have forgotten for the time being their own distinction between the immediate and the mediate, or that they regard the two as the same in Sense I, and to be treated as one. Certainly, in their reasonings upon this subject, men who hold to the two kinds of objects do confound them with one another, and strengthen their faith in the two by this misconception, as I shall show later. We have here, then, what we may call a kind of sameness, or pseudo-sameness, which deserves investigation, and which one should be careful not to confound with sameness of other kinds. Whether the word same is commonly applied in the premises is indifferent to my purpose. In the remainder of the present section I will consider the relation between the mental representative and its assumed correlatives.

SECOND: If we are to accept not merely the world of objects immediately known, but also a world or two worlds corresponding to this, and yet distinct from it, we cannot be sure our list of samenesses is complete unless we traverse in our search for the different kinds all the spheres of being in which we believe, and of which we think we can have some knowledge. In the section following this one I will try to discover the kinds of sameness which a believer in "external" things may reasonably attribute to them within their own sphere. In this there is no question of the relation of something in one sphere to a correlative something in another.

For the first point. What is in a man's mind when he is thinking of his percept as having a " real " object corresponding to it,

I have shown to be as follows: He has in mind an immediate object and a duplicate of this, not necessarily altogether like it, imagined as standing in a causal relation to it and represented by it. When it occurs to him that this imagined duplicate is itself an immediate object and not the "real" one, he does as much for it, and provides it with a similar duplicate. In every case, when he tries to think of an object immediately perceived as having a "real" correlate, he simply furnishes it with an imaginary double in this way. What else is he to do? He is trying to think of two objects; the "real" object cannot, it is said, be in the mind; he must then imagine it. If he is a Lockian he will have in mind the immediate object and two imaginary ones, one signifying the "real" object as a bundle of qualities, and the other, a highly vague one, picturing the "substance."

Now, since this is all that can be before the man's mind, any kind of sameness which concerns the percept and the "real" thing *must mean to him some relation between the immediate object and the image or images of which I have spoken.* When this is realized it is seen that we have here not a new kind of sameness, a distinct experience, but a kind already discussed. The relation between the immediate object and the images described is simply that between representative and thing represented. This I have already examined within the field of what is recognized as immediately known. Here, too, it would seem that we are in the field of the immediately known, since we have to do with percepts and ideas, but though these images are in this field, they are here, so to speak, under protest, and their framing is supposed to be justified[1] only by something assumed to be not in this field. When this something is thought of at all it is thought of in just the way I have described. This is what thinking it means. Nevertheless, this duplicate world is assumed to

---

[1] I have already pointed out the vagueness in this word.

be a world apart, and for this reason I have considered the sameness of percepts and their corresponding "real" objects by itself. It gives us sameness in sense seventh.

In writing the foregoing I have had in mind chiefly the position of the Lockian. I need not consider at length that taken by the Kantian, for what I have said will, with little change, apply to it also. If I hold to a "noumenon" as corresponding to my "phenomenon," and yet deny to it all qualities whatsoever, I must, to retain any appearance of consistency, represent it in my mind in the very vaguest possible way. Nevertheless, I must represent it, or I am not thinking of it at all, and I must relate the phenomenon and this vague representation in the way described. A true consistency would, of course, make impossible the whole process, for it would make impossible the giving of any quality at all to the representation, and the putting any relation between it and the phenomenon. In so dark a night cats do not merely turn grey, they disappear. On the other hand, if one is too liberal with this " noumenon," it palpably ceases to be a "noumenon," and degenerates into something very like a "phenomenon." The illusion must not be lost. Both these conflicting tendencies may be well illustrated in Mr. Spencer's "Unknowable." If we really refuse to allow to the consciousness of it "any qualitative or quantitative expression whatever,"[1] our vague image wholly disappears and there is nothing left in our consciousness but the "phenomenon." While if we follow the "First Principles" in coaxing it back into existence by allowing it reality,[2] and causality,[3] and a freedom from limits,[4] and printing its name with a capital letter,[5] as though it were even better than other things—if we do all this there is danger of the convalescent's becoming too

[1] First Principles. Part I, Chap. 4, § 26. N. Y., 1888, p. 91.

[2] *Ibid.* Chap. 4, § 24 ; Chap. 5, §§ 31, 32, *et passim.*

[3] *Ibid.* Chap. 5, § 31, *et passim.*

[4] *Ibid.* Chap. 4, § 24.   [5] *Ibid.* Chap. 5, § 32. *et passim.*

robust altogether. The problem has its parallel in the practical problem of paying wages:—one must not pay too little, or he loses his laborer; nor too much, or he loses his money. The thing is to find the happy mean which will keep an object of thought before a man's mind and yet not make him lose all appearance of consistency.

But in which ever of the ways mentioned a man thinks of "real" things, he does what I have described. And when he implies that the immediately known and the "real" are in some sense the same, as he does when he talks as if there were but the one object, or asserts that we do not know things as they are in themselves but only as they appear to us; he really uses the word same in the fifth sense that I have given. The fact that he is using it to indicate the relation between percepts and a certain class of ideas which he has come to regard as duplicates of his percepts does not make the use of the word a new one. Whatever may be the state of affairs outside of his consciousness, this is all that takes place within it; and the word same, used in this connection, can mean no more to him than I have said.

SEC. 9. To avoid needless prolixity I will class together and very briefly treat of the kinds of sameness which one may attribute to "external" things. It is not necessary to go at length into the discussion of these, for since the "external" world, as it is assumed by those who have faith in it, is, to the man thinking it, simply a more or less modified duplicate of the world of things immediately perceived; and since all ground for attributing to it any determinations at all must be found in that which is immediately perceived; we may naturally look to find in it nothing that we have not already found in this immediate world. How, indeed, could anything else get into it? We cannot have *in* mind what is by hypothesis *out* of mind. The "real" world is then, in the mind of the man who thinks it, a world of imagined objects, and the world of imagination depends for its material upon the world of sense. A little reflection will show that the kinds of sameness of these "realities" are only the kinds of sameness already discussed duplicated, and assumed to belong to a new world.

1. An "external" quality or group of qualities may be said to be the *same* with itself at any one instant. Here we have Sense I carried over into the field of imagined duplicates.

2. An "external" quality existing at one time may be said to be the *same* with an "external" quality existing at another time, to indicate that the two are similar. The same thing may be true of any group of qualities. Here we have Sense II.

3. The "external" bundle of qualities, which formed for Locke the knowable element in a thing or "body," may be regarded as being the *same* at two different times—as having, so to speak, a life-history. Here one is simply calling up in thought the experience described under Sense III.

4. Two "external" things (bundles of "real" qualities), or two "external" qualities, existing at one time, may be called the *same* to mark similarity. Here we have Sense IV.

5. An "external" thing (in the sense just indicated), or an "external" quality, may be called the *same* with its representative. If this representative be the immediate object of knowledge, we have the experience described as Sense VII. If it be another "external" thing or quality, *e. g.*, an "external" picture in an "external" mirror, an "external" statue in "external" marble, etc., we have Sense V.

6. Two men may be said to perceive the *same* "external" thing. In saying this one simply calls up in mind the complex described at length under VI, but makes the duplicate, which is, to him, the thing, stand in the complex in the place of the percept, this being now regarded as a mere representative.

7. An "external" thing may be said to be the *same* with its representative in consciousness or with the substance or noumenon assumed to underlie it.   Here we have Sense VII.

It would seem scarcely necessary to mention this last, since, if the representative in consciousness can be called the same with its "real" correlate, it would seem self-evident that the "real" correlate may be called the same with it.   I add it, however, for the sake of completeness.   It should be noted that in this last kind of sameness we step over the limits of any one class of being, ideas, things (as bundles of qualities), or substance.   The word is used to denote a relation between something in one class and a corresponding thing in another class.

In the foregoing I have been considering the sameness of "real" or "external" things regarded as bundles of qualities.   If one ask concerning the sameness of Locke's "substance," or the "noumenon" of other writers, I would say that our notions of this must vary with the kind of being we allow this nebulous entity.   Strict consistency in dealing with a noumenon as sometimes defined means, of course, its utter collapse.   If, however, we keep anything in mind at all, we must carry over to it at least the first of the kinds of sameness described.   I do not think it would be hard to show that several other kinds are carried over in despite of consistency by men who hold to this shadowy something under one name or another.

As, however, we do not find here any new sense of the word same, but mere repetition in a new field (if one may call it such), it seems unnecessary to dwell upon this part of my subject.

I have not discussed at all the sameness of things from the point of view of an adherent of that Natural Realism which claims that we know immediately real things and yet holds that real things are not our perceptions themselves, but something extra-mental.   This view is so incoherent that it is not likely to be taken seriously by men who have learned to reflect at all. I may say, however, *en passant*, that it does not add to the kinds of sameness I have described : it merely confounds them one with another, and falls into the inconsequences which naturally result from so doing.

SEC. 10. When we come to the question of the sameness of the Self or Ego we are, if possible, on more debatable ground than heretofore. The whole subject of our knowledge of the Self lies as yet, in the opinion of many, very much in the dark. Without undertaking the task of defining narrowly what this elusive something is, it would seem that I may safely make concerning it at least the following assertions :

In using the word self, we may have reference either to what is immediately known as appearing in the circle of consciousness, the phenomenon, or to a something supposed to lie beyond this sphere and to be known only through its representative in consciousness.

Now this something beyond may be looked at in various ways. John Locke, in discussing the not-self, made the three-fold division of idea, bundle of " real" qualities, and substance. He might with equal reason have distinguished in a similar way between the self as idea (the immediately known), the self as a bundle of " real" qualities (not immediately known), and the self as substance. As a matter of fact, however, he did not put the not-self and the self upon the same plane. He seemed to think that we know the self more immediately, and to hold that it enters consciousness as the bundle of " real" qualities[1] which, in the case of matter, is assumed to lie beyond. The " substance' of the self, however, he condemns to outer darkness and the company of material substance. To me there seems no reason, admitting the right to pass at all beyond the immediately per-

---

[1] Compare Bk. 4, Ch. 9, § 3 of the " Essay," with Bk. 4, Ch. 11, §§ 1, 4, 7, 8, and 9.

ceived, for making the distinction which he does make. And as
one, who has followed him with assent in his treatment of the
not-self, may with some justice complain of his inconsistency
and refuse to follow him here, I mention the position he might
have taken as well as the position he actually did take with
respect to the self and its existences.

SEC. 11. The word self may then be regarded as referring
either:

1. To the self as phenomenon, a something immediately perceived, a part or the whole of our conscious experience;

2. To a complex of "real" qualities beyond and represented
by the self as it appears in consciousness;

3. To the substance of self, or self as noumenon, a vague and
ill-defined something, supposed to be distinct from and to underlie phenomena or "real" qualities; or

4. To two, or to all, of these taken together.

If the word is used in the last of these senses any inquiry
concerning sameness must split up its complex meaning and treat
separately the different elements included. It remains, then, to
inquire what kinds of sameness we may attribute to the self in
the first three senses given. I will take them in reverse order.

SEC. 12. With respect to the third sense, which makes it
refer to the "substance" of Locke or the "noumenon" of other
writers: all the difficulties which arise out of the endeavor to
attribute sameness of any kind to any substance or noumenon
obtain here also. But it seems on the surface more glaringly
inconsistent in the adherent of noumena to discriminate between
different kinds as admitting of differences of treatment than it
does for him to suppose them capable of treatment at all.
Things that differ cannot be conceived as differing except in
qualities, and here there is question not of qualities but of
noumena. If one is to retain any appearance of consistency, he

must not maintain that the word same is applicable in any given sense to certain noumena and not to others. If he does so, he openly abandons his noumena to a phenomenal fate. And, as a matter of fact, I think it is plain that those believers in noumena, who distinguish them from one another, yet think of them in just the one way. If we take the utterances of a good representative of the class, Sir William Hamilton, we may see that although he distinguishes between the noumenal ego and the noumenal non-ego, not only do his clearest statements make such a distinction out of the question, but the distinction drawn is so vague and insignificant[1] that the two noumena may be thought of and reasoned about in the one way. Phenomena being abstracted, what was in his mind when he spoke of the one was probably in no respect different from what was in his mind when he spoke of the other. In so far, then, as the noumena themselves are concerned, it would seem that any kind of sameness which we may predicate of the noumenal not-self we may predicate on the same ground and with equal justice of the noumenal self, and *vice versa*. If, however, any sense of the word same marks a relation between a noumenon and some other thing or things, and if the two noumena differ as respects this relation, then this kind of sameness may be attributed to the one and not to the other. It may be claimed that we indicate just such a relation in using the word same in Sense VI ; and that, whatever one might do, one would under no circumstances speak of two men as perceiving the same self, noumenal or any other. I shall discuss this point when I come to discuss the sameness of self as phenomenon.

I may add here that when one obliterates the distinction between noumena by plunging them into the darkness of the "unknowable," there can, of course, be no question of a new sense

[1] Lectures on Metaphysics, VIII, N. Y., 1880, p. 97.

of the word same in the field I am discussing. On the general question of noumenal sameness, all that it seems to me necessary to say I have said before.

SEC. 13. The second sense of the word self would make it a complex of "real" qualities beyond, and represented by, the self as it appears in consciousness. Now, I do not think that the fact that one would attribute to the self, so considered, one class of qualities, and to the not-self another class, would, when the two "real" objects are considered in themselves, prevent one's ascribing to the former all the kinds of sameness which one may ascribe to the latter, or would justify the assumption of a new kind of sameness proper only to the former. In discussing the sameness of "external" things I have not made any one kind of it dependent upon the peculiar quality of their qualities, if I may so speak. I considered them only as groups of qualities in general, supposed to be external to consciousness. The idea of the "real" self is in its general character essentially similar to that of the "real" not-self. Provided that the two classes of qualities have enough in common to be properly called qualities, and to be capable of being related to each other in groups, they may differ in kind *toto cœlo* without necessitating a difference of treatment from the point of view with which I am at present concerned. It is very evident, however, that those who have thought of the self as a "real" thing, distinct from consciousness, and yet to be in some way intelligibly represented in thought, have had a tendency to represent it very much as they have represented material objects. There has been a general effort to get rid of the idea of extension, but this has been shown rather in reducing the size of the object and attributing to it inconsistent space relations than in denying it such relations altogether. Bishop Butler's argument for immortality from the indiscerptibility of the uncompounded shows that he thought of the self as he thought of a material atom,[1] and Sir William Hamilton's scholastic notion of the ubiquity of the soul in the bodily organism—"all in the whole and all in every part"[2]—makes it sufficiently clear that he thought of it so, too ; though, to be sure, such ubiquity would make of it a very queer atom indeed. If, then, the man, who holds to the self in the second sense of the word, calls up in using the word a mental complex like that which represents to him a " real" not-self, there is all the more reason why we should not expect to find anything in his thought which would suggest a new kind of sameness within the sphere of the " real" self. It remains, of course, to notice here, as in the case of the noumenal self, that any sense of the word same which has reference not so much to the things under discussion as to the relations of these things to other things, may, if self and not-self differ as to these relations, be applicable to the one and not to the other. Thus Sense VI may be regarded as inapplicable to the "real" self. I will discuss this point more fully in a few moments. With this one exception we may, therefore, I think, apply the kinds of sameness enumerated under Sec. 9 as obtaining in the sphere of "external" things to the "real" self also, and it would seem that no new kinds are to be added. It is unnecessary to repeat here the classification already given.

Sec. 14. We come finally to the self as a something immediately perceived, the self as phenomenon or idea. I do not mean to use these names in a question-begging way, and I will try to exhaust all reasonable possibilities in discussing it and its samenesses.

Now, whatever the self is, it would seem that it must be, in

---

[1] "Analogy," Part I. Chap. I.

[2] Lectures on Metaphysics, XXV., N. Y., 1880, p. 356. Hamilton's utterances concerning "reality" are incoherent, and inconsistent. I do him no injustice, however, if I give the above as "one of his views."

so far as it is a thing immediately known, either a part or the whole of consciousness, or one or the other of these regarded in some peculiar aspect or relation.

If it be a part of consciousness, recognized as distinct from another part, the non-ego, we may reasonably maintain :

1. That the perceived self is at any moment what it is—is the same with itself. The question whether it be simple and unanalyzable does not affect the problem. This is sameness in sense I.

2. That if it be simple and unanalyzable, this simple element of consciousness may be the same at two different times, and if complex, two elements or two complexes of elements, belonging to different times may be the same. This is sameness in sense II.

3. That if we regard the self as an object having a life-history, as consisting of successive elements united in a series as sense elements are united in the series which is for us a material object (immediately known), we may speak of its being the same on two successive days, even though it exhibit dissimilar qualities, primary reference being had not to likeness of elements, but to the experience which has been described at length in discussing sense III.

4. That we may speak of two selves, of two elements of two selves (if selves be complex), or of two elements of one self (if one self may contain two such elements), as at any one time the same, to indicate that they are similar. This is sameness in sense IV. It should be kept in mind, however, that we never look upon one consciousness as containing two selves as it contains one self, or as it may contain two material objects (immediately known). The second self in mind is recognized as present only as an imagined object. Nevertheless it would seem quite proper to use the word same to mark this relation of similarity between the perceived self and an imagined self, just as we use

it to mark a likeness of two material objects, or of one material object and the memory image of such an object.

5. That we may speak of the self and its representative as the same. The memory image of a later time may stand for the self as experienced at an earlier. Unless it be claimed that yesterday's consciousness of self is actually to-day's consciousness, one must admit that the self remembered is the self known through its proxy. And one may in his reasonings about the self use as a symbol the pronoun " I," paying little attention as he goes along to what it stands for, and yet knowing it may serve in place of the obscure something it represents. These are instances of sameness in sense V.

6. That we never use the word same in sense VI in speaking of the self as we do in speaking of the not-self. We do not say two men perceive the same self as we say they perceive the same tree or house. The familiar distinction between the subjective and the objective marks out the latter as in a sense, peculiar to itself, common and impersonal.

I have already shown what we have in mind when we say two men see the same material thing. We have a picture of the thing, and of the bodies of the two men in a certain relation to it ; and we imagine a copy of the thing as in some way connected with each of these bodies, and due to its relation to the thing. When relations to a material object are in question all the bodies in a consciousness are on a par. We may directly perceive the one thing and two or more bodies holding similar relations to it. But it is not so in the case of selves. The one self that we find in each consciousness seems to be peculiarly related to one body to the exclusion of others. And as we have not, in the case of this self, the conditions which led us to mark the similar relations of two human bodies (our representatives of the men) to one material object, by saying two men see the same thing, we, of course, do not say that two men see the same self. The word same, in sense VI, we may regard, then, as inapplicable to the self as immediately known.[1] This appears to be due, however, not to the nature of this self in itself considered, but to its peculiar relation to the other things in a consciousness.

Moreover, since the other two selves, the self as group of "real" qualities and the self as noumenon, are to us, as it were, shadows cast by the self immediately known—assumed to exist only because this is known to exist, and thought of as "present" only because this is known to be present—since, I say, these two selves hold in our thought this peculiar relation of dependence upon the self in consciousness, it is to be expected that we never find any one speaking of two men as seeing the same "real" self as one might readily speak of two men as seeing the same "real" tree. One says he has evidence that two men see the same "real" tree, when he has or can have in consciousness an immediately perceived tree and two immediately perceived human bodies in a certain relation to it. If no one had ever had this experience in the sphere of the immediately known, we have no reason to think any one would ever have thought of applying the phrase in question to a tree mediately known. And as we do not have a similar experience touching the self in consciousness, it is only natural to find that no one applies the phrase to any self out of consciousness. When things differ their shadows ought to differ too. Sameness in sense VI we may regard, then, as not attributable to self in any of the three senses of the word.

7. That, finally, there seems no more reason why one should not call the self as immediately known the same with the self as

---

[1] Owing to the ambiguity already pointed out as existing in terms which stand for our objects of knowledge and our knowledge of these objects, it would seem almost impossible to avoid misconception without unendurable reiteration. In the above paragraph, by the words "body," "object," "self," etc., I always refer to things immediately known.

"external" thing, or with the self as noumenon, than the not-self as similarly perceived the same with the not-self as similarly inferred. The supposed relationships are in the two cases exactly alike. Here we have sameness in sense VII.

SEC. 15. If we claim that by the self as immediately known we understand not a part but the whole of consciousness, we should seem, unless we in some way modify our statement, to obliterate the distinction between self and not-self. Still, taking the words simply, and assuming that we mean by self all that is immediately known, we do not find that this will necessitate any important difference in the discussion of its samenesses. Consciousness as a whole is certainly what it is, or the same with itself, at any instant: two elements in it belonging to different times, or two complexes of elements belonging to different times may be the same, as being alike; it may be regarded as having a life history, and may from this point of view be called the same at different times without regard to similarity; two simultaneous elements or complexes of elements in it may be called the same to mark the fact that they resemble each other, or it, as a whole, may for the same reason be called the same with another consciousness (imagined); it and its representative (for example, the memory-image of its former self), may be called the same; and we may use the word same to indicate its relation to its supposed "real" correlate in an extra-consciousness world, whether we make this "thing" or "noumenon."

It will be observed that in the preceding I have allowed the self, considered as the whole of consciousness, all the kinds of sameness upon my list except the sixth. There is, however, no objection, except that arising from oddity of expression, against allowing it this kind of sameness too. If we really mean by the self the whole of consciousness, then everything immediately perceived is a part of the self. If then, it is proper to say two men see the same tree, one may go on to say, if one choses, that two men see a part of the one self. Such an expression could, of course, be used only in speaking of the objective part of this self, the part which those who distinguish between ego and non-ego call the not-self. It is needless to say that no one ever thinks of talking in this way. I merely mention the point for the sake of completeness in my analysis.

SEC. 16. If by the self we do not understand a part or the whole of consciousness taken simply, but the one or the other of these regarded from some peculiar point of view, does it affect the question of the kinds of sameness we may attribute to it? It may be asserted, for example, that when we are thinking of the world of things immediately perceived as conditioned by its relation to a particular organism (also immediately perceived)— as duplicated by a pressure on the eyes, as annihilated by a blow on the head—we make these things mental, and properly include them under the head of self; whereas, when we abstract these same things in thought from the organism, and, so to speak, objectify them, we properly include them under the head of not-self. We are thus to regard the one thing as an element of the self or of the not-self, according to the light in which it is viewed. But it does not seem to me that if we take the word self in the sense just described, or in any analogous sense, we need alter the list of samenesses already given. We are still considering a part or the whole of consciousness, and the fact that we are viewing it in one light rather than another would not apparently influence in any way its kinds of sameness.

SEC. 17. This would certainly appear to be the case if we take the words *part* and *whole* of consciousness in their common acceptation, as denoting a portion or the totality of mental elements (sensations, feelings, volitions, ideas), in their various relations to each other. It remains, however, to consider a position, which, it may be claimed, is not covered by the foregoing classification of possible positions, when the words "part" and "whole" are thus understood. Suppose that one distinguishes in the Kantian fashion between the *form* and the *matter* of what appears in consciousness, and maintains that the formal element, the arrangement, or "unity" of consciousness is to be attributed to mind, or, if you please, is mind, and for "mind" I may here write "self," while the matter or content, the raw material to be elaborated and related, is to be distinguished from this as a thing apart. Can it be shown that the above given kinds of sameness have significance in regard to the self so understood? Whether we call this a *part* of consciousness or not will depend on our use of terms. It is not a part, as commonly understood, nor is it the whole of consciousness.

Now, it has seemed to me that those who have laid most emphasis upon this formal element in consciousness have been very vague in their treatment of it. On the part of many writers there is little evidence of even an attempt at scientific exactitude. And yet it does not appear that the subject admits of treatment only in this loose and unsatisfactory way. If we can discuss it at all, there seems no reason why, with increasing knowledge, we may not expect to discuss it with accuracy and precision.

If we consider this formal element of consciousness in a concrete instance, it may help us to classify our ideas concerning it. Let us imagine three points in such relations to each other that when each is connected with the other two by straight lines we have an equilateral triangle. The three points are, of course, what they are at any instant. And whatever a relation may be, if the mutual relations of these three points are capable of being considered apart from the points, as a distinct element in consciousness, there appears no reason why we should not assert with equal justice that these relations are what they are at any instant. When we take note of the points we take note of the relations, and we do not confound the one with the other.

And just as I may say that such a set of three points imagined or observed now is the same with another and a similar set imagined or observed at some former time, meaning by the word same to indicate similarity, and not sameness in the strict sense mentioned just above; so there appears no reason at all why I may not say that the mutual relations of the one set of points are the same with the mutual relations of the other, making here, too, the distinction between sameness in the former, stricter, sense, and sameness in this second sense of similarity. If what is contained in a consciousness at any one instant, is, *ipso facto*, to be distinguished from what is contained in it at any other instant, there seems equal reason for making this distinction in the material element and in the formal. It is quite true that men are not accustomed to carrying this distinction into the region of form. The whole history of the dispute as to universals is evidence of the way in which men have confounded the kinds of sameness; but I fancy that even those who would clearly recognize that red color imagined yesterday and red color imagined to-day are the same merely in being similar, or in standing in a relation of original and representative, would yet not think of distinguishing triangularity noticed yesterday from triangularity noticed to-day, and marking that they are not the same in the first and strictest sense of the word. And yet it would be hard to show why two indistinguishably similar color sensations, existing in consciousness at different times, are to be kept apart in thought and recognized as two sensations, while two occurrences of the consciousness of triangularity (I use the clumsy phrase to avoid any question-begging word), are not to be distinguished as separate in a similar way. To say that the formal element is not a thing, but an activity, does not alter the position. If an activity is enough of a thing to be talked about and distinguished from other things, we may surely recognize an activity in consciousness yesterday as numerically different from an activity in consciousness to-day.

Furthermore, if, instead of taking as simple an instance of form as the relations of the three points I have been discussing, I choose to take the sum total of the relations between the material elements (here I use *material* as correlative to *formal*), which go to make up the life history of a material object, say a tree, why may I not speak of the formal tree as being the same at two times, meaning thereby that the group of relations co-existent at any one time may be regarded as representative of any other group belonging to the one series or of the whole series? To be sure, I am not justified by common usage in thus speaking, since common usage marks only distinctions which are practically important, and by the words "the same tree" includes both form and matter. Nevertheless, I can see no reason why, if this element of form does admit of being considered apart, it is not at least possible to find in this field the kind of sameness we have in mind when we say that we have seen on two successive days the same tree.

Again, if I can speak of two simultaneous sensations of redness in one consciousness (*c. g.*, the two halves of a red surface), as the same, meaning to indicate simply similarity, why may I not also speak of two simultaneous "experiences of triangularity" in one consciousness as the same, and keep clearly in mind here, too, that I mean only to indicate similarity? If I can speak of a sensation or a complex of sensations in one consciousness as the same with a similar sensation or group of sensations in another, and yet not forget that I am dealing with two things, why may I not do as much for two similar relations or groups of relations in two consciousnesses? If in the one case I do not confound sameness in the sense of similarity with sameness of the kind we mean when we say each thing is at each instant the same with itself, why should I do so in the other case? If, I repeat, the formal element in consciousness is enough of a thing to be distinguished from the material element and discussed, there appears no reason why it should not be open to distinctions of this kind.

And when I call up in memory a triangle once seen, the memory image would seem to stand as a representative of the original in both its elements, form and matter. In neither should the representative be confounded with the original. If we may use the word same to indicate this peculiar relation of representation between two things yet recognized as two, it would seem only just to allow this distinction as much in the case of triangularity as in the case of redness or blueness.

As to the sixth kind of sameness. May we grant this to the self, if by self we mean the formal element of consciousness? I have said a little way back, before taking up the distinction of formal and material, that, if we make the word self cover all the immediately known, there is nothing to prevent one's saying that two men see a part of the same self, for material objects (immediately known) would have to be regarded as such parts. And here it is evident that if we make self to cover the whole of the formal element in a consciousness, it of course includes the formal element in what we may call the objective side of consciousness—the side which is, in some sense of the words, common and impersonal. Now, we do say that two men see the same tree, and by tree, the man who distinguishes between form and matter means a certain complex containing both formal and material elements. These elements he believes he can distinguish from one another, and pay attention predominantly now to the one, and now to the other. Does it not seem to follow that a man may as truly be said to see the formal element as the material, and that two men who see the same tree may with justice be said to see the same shape or arrangement of parts? In other words, may we not apply the sixth sense of the word same to the formal element in consciousnesss if this element is a thing capable of treatment at all? And if this formal element in a tree seen by two men is a part of the self, why may we not say that two men see a part of the same self, even though we make self mere form? It would sound very odd to say so, of course, but that should not weigh with a philosopher, if consistency require it.

Finally, if I may call an immediately perceived object the same with its supposed "external" correlate, not confounding the two, but merely marking by the word a peculiar instance of the representative relation, why may I not, if I believe that "external" things stand in "real" relations to each other truly represented by our perceptions of things and their relations—why, in this case, may I not speak of the relations, "external" and "internal," as the same, without on that account forgetting that I am pointing out a relation between two things (if I may thus speak of relations), numerically different? Are they not as different as the "matter" of consciousness and its correlate in the "outer" world?

SEC. 18. In the foregoing I have endeavored to make my list of the kinds of sameness complete. I can think of nothing that has been overlooked ; but as I have been trying to force a path through a thicket few have made any sustained effort to penetrate, it is quite possible my map of the ground may need emendation. I shall be very glad of any criticism which will help me to improve it. And as the many divisions made, and the many distinctions drawn, may very possibly tend to produce in one who has followed the discussion thus far, a state of mind akin to that of the "true-begotten" Gobbo, when he was obligingly directed to the Jew's house by his hopeful son, a short summary of the results obtained may serve to facilitate apprehension and intelligent criticism.

What has been done is this :

I began by considering the kinds of sameness of things immediately known, leaving out of consideration for the time being the sameness of the self or ego. This resulted in the following kinds :

I. Any mental element or complex of mental elements may be said to be the same with itself at any instant.

II. Any mental element or complex of mental elements in existence at one time may be called the same with a mental element or complex of mental elements existing at another time, to indicate that the two are similar.

III. We may say that we perceive the same object (complex of mental elements) at two different times, when we do not mean that what is actually experienced on the two occasions is the same in either of the preceding senses; but only that the two experiences are terms in a certain series, the whole of which may be regarded as represented by any part. In this sense does one see the same tree on two succeeding days.

IV. Any two mental elements or complexes of mental elements in consciousness at the one time may be called the same to mark the fact that they are alike.

V. Any mental element or complex of mental elements may be called the same with its representative, whether this representative resemble it or not.

VI. When a man has learned from experience of his own body (as a thing immediately known) that a consciousness of his body in a certain peculiar relation to a given object (complex of mental elements) is a presupposition to a consciousness of the object, and wishes to mark the fact that he is perceiving or imagining two human bodies in this relation to a single object, and connecting in thought with each of them a picture of the object, he may say that he is perceiving or imagining two men seeing the same object. This sense of the word same obviously expresses quite a complex thought.

VII. In addition to these kinds of sameness found within the sphere of the immediately known, we obtain one kind by stepping beyond it, which, since we step beyond it, so to speak, with only one foot, may be here mentioned as belonging at least partially to the world of immediate objects. When we have come to believe that things in consciousness have their correlates in a world outside of consciousness, we may speak of the things in consciousness as the same with their "external" correlates; or, at any rate, we may talk of them as if they were the same in some sense of the word which will allow us to include the two (or three) distinct things under one name, and treat them as one. This is constantly done. The importance of remembering that we have really more than one thing to consider, it would seem scarcely necessary to emphasize. How far this is really a new kind of sameness I discussed at some length.

After having marked these seven kinds of sameness as having to do with the immediately known, I proceeded to consider the kinds of sameness which may obtain in a world or worlds beyond consciousness. It was pointed out that one may look upon the "external" in three ways. One may believe in "external" things as merely bundles of "real" qualities, and may stop there : or one may believe in such bundles of "real" qualities, and in addition hold to "substance" or "substratum" as an obscure something implied by these "real" qualities : or, lastly, one may hold that the only correlate of the thing in consciousness is "noumenon," a thing not distinguishable from the "substance" above mentioned.

It was then shown that a realm of "external" things, consisting of bundles of "real" qualities in a world beyond consciousness, would, since it is to the man thinking it merely a duplicate of the immediate world, admit of the existence of all the kinds of sameness above enumerated, and would not furnish any one kind which might increase the list. And with respect to the "external" as noumenon, it was stated that if the noumenal be represented to the mind at all, at least the first kind of sameness must be attributed to it, and that other kinds will be, in proportion to the degree of clearness allowed this vague and inconsistent entity. No new kind of sameness need, however, be looked for in this field. If one hold to the "external" in both kinds, he must, of course, search three distinct realms of being before he can be sure that he has not overlooked any legitimate sense of the word same. As a result of the foregoing analysis we may maintain that, whatever be his belief as to ideas, things, and noumena, his search will not result in more than the seven kinds of sameness I have given. In the assumed new fields we find mere repetition. The pure Idealist would reduce the list to six by dropping off the seventh kind altogether.

Next, as to the sameness of the Self or Ego. It was pointed out that one may take the word self to mean: (1) the self in consciousness, or as phenomenon; (2) the self as bundle of "real" qualities out of consciousness; (3) the self as "substance" or "noumenon;" (4) two of these, or all of these, taken together.

It was said that as the fourth sense is sufficiently discussed in examining the first three, it would not be separately considered. The three remaining senses were then taken up in reverse order.

The third and the second were found to furnish no new kind of sameness, and to be on a par with the corresponding senses of the word "not-self," except as touching the sixth kind of sameness. As respects this, it was admitted that no one would speak of two men as perceiving the same self, whether as bundle of " real" qualities or as noumenon. It was remarked, however, that this is due not to a difference in the self and not-self in themselves considered, but to a difference in their relation to other things in a consciousness.

The self in consciousness, or as immediately known, was then discussed. It was stated that we may safely assume this to be either a part or the whole of consciousness, or the one or the other of these in some·peculiar aspect or relation. Self, viewed as a part of consciousness, was found to furnish no new kind of sameness, and was found to admit of all the kinds discovered except the sixth ; this one being inadmissible from the fact that when we make the self a part of consciousness we always make it the subjective part and not the objective. Self, viewed as the whole of consciousness, was likewise found to furnish no new kind of sameness, and it was found to admit of all the seven kinds discovered—even of the sixth, though in a modified way, since this kind can belong only to a part of the self, the objective part, which is in some sense common and impersonal. It may, to be sure, be objected that it would be contrary to common usage to speak of two men as seeing the same self in any sense of that word ; but in making the self the whole of consciousness one has already abandoned the common standpoint, and one may as well be consistent in carrying out the consequences. Assuming the self to be not a part or the whole of consciousness simply, but regarded in some peculiar aspect or relation, was not found to be significant as concerns kinds of sameness.

It still remained to consider a possible position; that of the man who distinguishes between the formal and the material element in consciousness, and identifies self or mind with the former. The formal element of consciousness is not a part of consciousness as the word part is commonly used, nor is it the whole of consciousness, in the ordinary acceptation of the word whole. And though this view might very well have been brought under a former head by stretching a little the meaning of the word part, yet such is its importance that I chose rather to omit it when discussing self as a part of consciousness (there using the word part in a limited sense), and to take it up later by itself.

It was insisted that if the formal element in consciousness is enough of a thing to be distinguished from something else, and to be discussed, it is enough of a thing to admit of distinctions and differences much as other things do. After examination it appeared, as a matter of fact, that there is no reason why the believer in "form" should not attribute to it all of the seven kinds of sameness before described—even (in the modified way described a moment ago) the sixth kind. And it also appeared that no new kind of sameness is discoverable in this field. With this closed the search for samenesses.

It will be observed that we have passed in review the self and the not-self as immediately known, the self and the not-self as bundles of "real" qualities out of consciousness, and the self and the not-self as noumenon or substance. I know of no other field in which the search may be prosecuted, unless such be invented gratuitously by increasing the "layers" of being in a way no one seems inclined to increase them. And in view of the fact that the samenesses found in any "layer" below the first seem to be only repetitions of what we find in that one, we could have no reason to hope that any such needless increase in strata could add a single new kind of sameness to those described.

Sec. 19. Now that we have obtained a list of the different kinds of sameness, we may pass our eye over it with a view to discovering what the various kinds have in common, and what is the reason that we express such diverse experiences by the use of the one word. Such an examination reveals the fact that the common notion which unites them is the idea of similarity. In some cases this notion lies more in the foreground than in others, but in all cases it is present, and forms the bond of union. I will run through the list and point this out, beginning, however, with the second kind, and reserving the first for discussion after the others.

II. A mere mention of the second kind of sameness is, in this connection, sufficient. Two mental experiences are there avowedly called the same to mark similarity.

III. When we speak of the same object as perceived on two occasions, we do not, as has been noticed, mean that what is actually in the sense at the two different times is similar. Nevertheless, we find here, too, the notion of similarity, for the two experiences are not considered merely in themselves, but as elements in a group or series, and as each representing the whole series. When, therefore, we have the two experiences, we regard ourselves as having in them two experiences of the one series ; which means, to be more explicit, that we have in mind on the two occasions two complexes which are similar, and which, when thought of together, are related to each other as the memory image and its original are related. Here the likeness lies in what is represented, not in the representatives.

IV. As in the second kind of sameness, so in the fourth, the reference to similarity is unmistakable. We call qualities or things the same when they are of the one kind, when they are observed to resemble each other.

V. The relation of representative and thing represented evidently implies the notion of similarity. It is quite true that we often recognize as in this relation things that we do not think of as being similar at all, and yet a little reflection will show that one thing can stand for another only *in so far* as it resembles it. The resemblance may lie in the qualities of the things in themselves considered, or it may lie in external relations of which the things are capable, or functions which they may serve. The very notion of a proxy is a something which, for the purpose in hand, may be regarded as capable of assuming the functions of another. In so far as it can do this it is like the other. Things wholly different (if things could be wholly different) could not represent each other.

VI. When a man thinks of two other men as perceiving the same object, he must recognize, if he reflect, that he has in mind a picture of the object, of two human bodies in a peculiar relation to it, and two images of the object somehow connected with these bodies. He need not think of these images as wholly resembling his picture of the object or each other. He does, indeed, make them more or less like his picture of the object, but what is prominent in his mind is the thought of them as representatives, as related to and giving information concerning the object. I say concerning the object, but this phrase is ambiguous. If the man under discussion believes in "real" objects in an extra-consciousness world, he will look upon the images as representing such a "real" object; though, of course, his guarantee for this "real" object, and all his information concerning, it must be found in his picture of the object, and this, or its copy, will stand for the "real" object in any mental complex he may construct. If the man be an Idealist, accepting only what can be found in a consciousnesss, he will look upon the two images as related to his picture of the object and representative of that. In any case he must regard them as representatives, and in this sense the same with the thing they represent. The notion of similarity which is at the bottom of this idea of representative and thing represented is then implied in sameness of the sixth kind also.

VII. And since those who distinguish between the immediate and the mediate objects of knowledge make the former representative of the latter, we have evidently this implied notion of similarity in the seventh kind of sameness as well as in the sixth. The mediate object is said to be known *through* the immediate: that is, the qualities and relations of the one are made to stand for and serve in place of the qualities and relations of the other. This they can do, of course, only in so far as the two sets of qualities and relations are similar. It is easy enough to see that this notion of similarity is present when we think of an idea or complex of ideas as representing a "real" thing beyond consciousness, and giving information concerning it. When, however, we sublimate our "real" thing into a noumenon and strip it of the determinations which, taken together, make up our idea of a thing, we destroy, if we are consistent and thorough-going, all notion of similarity between the two; but in doing this we destroy our noumenon altogether. If, for instance, we refuse to allow to our notion of a thing "any qualitative or quantitative expression whatever," we cannot think of the thing as having reality or existence, or any mark by which it is to be distinguished from nothing at all. In this case the idea is no longer representative, for it has nothing to represent. If, on the other hand, we do not wholly destroy the noumenon, but still allow it a diluted existence of an indefinite kind, in so far as it has this, and can be represented in mind at all, it resembles the idea, and just so far may the idea stand as its representative.

I have already pointed out that several of those who pin their faith to "external" realities seem to apprehend at times but dimly, if at all, that the relation of phenomenon and noumenon, or of idea and "real" thing, is that of representative and thing represented, and that we have here two things and not one. Certainly they sometimes pass from one to the other without rhyme or reason, and apparently in complete unconsciousness of the fact that they have made any change at all. If, for the time being, they really take the two for one, they are not thinking of the seventh kind of sameness, but of another kind. As this is done through mere inadvertence and looseness of reasoning, and cannot be justified on their own assumptions, it is not worth while to dwell upon it farther. Where one really has in mind the seventh kind of sameness, the elements I have mentioned will be found in it.

I. Finally, we come to the perplexing case that I postponed at the outset. What has sameness of the first kind in common with the rest? How can we speak of similarity when strictly one thing is in question? Not one thing in the loose sense in which we call a material object one thing in its successive states, nor one in the sense in which the memory image and its original are one, but one thing as a single element of knowledge is itself at any one instant? How can the idea of likeness hold here? Dundreary's bird flocking all by itself would seem to have found its philosophical prototype.

It may be said that though the thing in question is strictly one, yet we divide it from itself in thought and then affirm it of itself. We give expression to the logical law of identity by saying that x is x. But here the difficulty meets us that, if we are really talking about only the one x, we have said quite all we have to say in merely saying x; while if, to complete our thought, we must add the second x, we have not an identical proposition, in any strict sense of the word, but a synthetic one. It is easy enough in words to divide a "thing" from "itself," since the words "thing" and "itself" are two, and may readily be distinguished. In the same way it is easy in words to affirm a thing to be and not to be at the one time. There is no law to prevent one's stringing sounds together as he may please. But if one is interested not in the mere symbols, but in that which they are supposed to represent, one must see that the expression "x is x," to be a significant proposition, must have a subject and a predicate, and affirm a relation between them. Here we have, by hypothesis, strictly one thing for subject and predicate. The proposition "x is x" must then consist of one thing and a relation between it—which is about as significant as the statement that a door may consist of one side and a relation between it. Between what? One side.[1] Every form of proposition employed to give expression to the law of identity implies this difficulty. Whether we say "x is x," or "whatever is is," or "everything is identical with itself," our proposition, taken literally, is either useless (since we have said all we have to say in mentioning the subject alone), or untrue (since we add a new element in adding the predicate).

[1] This abnormal door has its parallel in the now discredited *causa sui*. Note the following from Descartes: " De même, lorsque nous disons que Dieu est par soi, nous pouvons aussi à la vérité entendre cela négativement, comme voulant dire qu'il n'a point de cause; mais si nous avons auparavant recherché la cause pourquoi il est ou pourquoi il ne cesse point d'être, et que, considérant l' immense et incompréhensible puissance qui est contenue dans son Idée, nous l'ayons reconnue si pleine et si abondante qu' en effet elle soit la vraie cause pourquoi il est, et pourquoi il continue ainsi toujours d'être, et qu' il n'y en puisse avoir d'autre que celle-là, nous disons que Dieu est *par soi*, non plus négativement, mais au contraire très-positivement. Car, encore qu'il n'est pas besoin de dire qu'il est la cause efficiente de soi-même, de peur que peut-être on n'entre en dispute du mot ; néanmoins, parce que vous voyons que ce qui fait qu'il est par soi, ou qu'il n'a point de cause différente de soi-même, ne procède pas du néant, mais de la réelle et véritable immensité de sa puissance, il nous est tout à fait loisible de penser qu'il fait en quelque façon la même chose à l'égard de soi-même que la cause efficiente à l'égard de son effet, et partant qu'il est par soi positivement."—Réponses aux Premières Objections.

It is then sufficiently evident that the forms used to express the logical law of identity do not, taken strictly, express at all the kind of sameness with which we are now concerned, but, on the contrary, something very different. We are considering a sameness in which there is no duality whatever, but our expressions would seem to have no meaning except as indicating a relation between two. They are then significant, not as *expressing* sameness of the first kind, but as *suggesting* it, and this they certainly serve to do. The reason for this I shall try to give in a moment.

It has been said that in the other kinds of sameness we always find the notion of similarity. When, however, we distinguish two things as two and yet recognize them as similar, we must have what I may call a mixed experience of likeness and unlikeness. In any two things compared, the degrees of likeness and unlikeness may vary, and we may fix attention upon similarities or differences. In proportion to the attention given to dissimilar elements will the two objects be clearly distinguished from each other and discriminated as two. If the purpose in hand does not require a careful attention to differences, and if what is prominent in mind is the likeness of the two objects, the sense of duality may fall into the background, and the man pass readily from one object to the other with little consciousness that he has made a change. As I now look at the two ink-stands on my desk, I clearly recognize them as two and yet as of the one kind. Here I am as distinctly aware that they are two as I am that they are in some respects the same. But in some of the kinds of sameness I have described this sense of duality falls more into the shade. When I speak of seeing the same ink-stand twice, or when I call up in memory an ink-stand once seen, I am likely, unless I take particular pains to reflect upon my mental operation, to have but a dim realization of the fact that I have two distinct things to deal with. How those who distinguish between the immediate and the mediate objects of knowledge have a tendency to forget their distinction, and to pass unconsciously from one to the other, I have dwelt upon sufficiently.

Suppose, now, that from two objects' which we recognize as similar and yet distinct, we abstract one by one the elements which differ. So long as there is any difference left, we still have "identity in diversity"—similarity in the ordinary sense of the term, which implies a recognition of two things as two. When, however, the last difference disappears, all sense of duality must disappear with it, for any division or distinction within what remains is inadmissible. Things which are distinguished are distinguished through some difference. A sense of duality implies a discrimination between two, and where it is impossible to discriminate duality vanishes. Similarity, as we commonly use the word, must then disappear with the disappearance of all dissimilarity between two objects. I say " between two objects" in default of a better expression, for, of course, we have at this point no longer two objects. My meaning is, however, sufficiently plain. A sense of duality implies difference, and similarity, as commonly understood, implies duality. The similarity will then take itself off with the last difference.

It may be objected that *a consciousness of duality* and *a consciousness of similarity* are only possible on the ground that I mention, but that duality and similarity themselves may really obtain when no difference between two is perceptible. But a moment's reflection will make it plain that one who speaks thus is simply supplying in himself the elements that he is supposing absent in the case of another. If he uses the words "duality" and "similarity," and they really mean anything to him, they imply all that I have said. He cannot represent to himself two things at all without distinguishing them from each other, and he can not distinguish them from each other unless they differ in some way. If, then, he speak of two things as being two and yet completely indistinguishable, he is, taken literally, talking nonsense. He may, of course, mean the misleading phrase to be understood as indicating something not actually expressed by the words. He may mean to point out that, under certain circumstances, in which he has an experience which he calls a recognition of two objects as two and as similar, he has reason to think another mind has an experience partly like and partly unlike his own—like in as much as it contains what corresponds to that which is *common* to the two objects he has in mind ; unlike in as much as it contains nothing which corresponds to the elements which make it possible for him to recognize *two* objects. It is this that is in his mind when he speaks of thinking of two objects as really two and yet indistinguishable to this man or that. If, however, the expression "two things may be indistinguishable" is used to indicate this experience, it should be carefully borne in mind that the proposition must not be taken literally, for the good reason that the subject and predicate are not in the one consciousness. The "two objects" are in the mind of Smith, and the "indistinguishable" element in the mind of Jones. When we speak of two men as seeing the same thing, I have shown that we are using the word same in a looser sense which should never be confounded with the stricter sense. Strictly speaking, then, the "two things" are never indistinguishable, but that which corresponds to the two things in a consciousness from which all recognition of duality is absent. That one man may have a consciousness of duality while another man has not, and that these two experiences may be related as the experiences of different minds are related when we say they are experiencing the same thing, no one would care to dispute. Should a man say that he can think of himself as unable to distinguish two things which are nevertheless two, the case would not be materially different. The man cannot, of course, think of *the two things* as indistinguishable, but he may think of two things and connect with this thought the thought of himself as having an experience in which there is no consciousness of duality.

But, it may be insisted, we are still only talking about consciousness; let us come to "real" things. Suppose no one able to distinguish between them, abstract all consciousness of difference, would not two "real" things remain two, however we might confound them? Can a thing in one place be a thing in another place, however closely it may resemble it, or however ignorant we may be?

To this I answer that when one speaks of *two* "real" things the words only mean something to him because he has present in mind what I have said must be present if one is to have a consciousness of duality. A "thing in one place" and a "thing in another place" are to him two simply because he thinks them as differing—in place. When one has come to the conclusion that he must duplicate his experience, distinguish between the world of immediate and the world of mediate objects, and place the latter in a region "outside," there is nothing to prevent him from thinking of two "real" things as two, although all distinctions within the field of immediate objects have been obliterated. Still, in thinking these "real" things as two, he does just what he does in thinking two immediate objects as two—he recognizes difference. The twoness depends upon difference as much in the one case as in the other, and to speak of two objects in a "real" world as two and yet having no differing element would be to use words without meaning. In talking about a "real" world, if we are really to talk and not merely to utter a series of sounds, our words must be significant. To say "this or that may be in a 'real' world, though we may not be able to conceive it," would, if "this" or "that" implies a contradiction, be to say nothing. The fact is that this "external" world, as we think it, implies the notions of before and after, in this place and that, all the distinctions and differences which make it to us a world of distinct objects. Of course it follows that things in the "external" world are thought as distinct from each other, but this does not affect my statement that distinction is impossible without difference.

We may, then, have a series of experiences, beginning with one in which two objects are recognized as similar and yet are very clearly distinguished as two objects, continued in others in which the sense of duality falls more and more into the background, and ending in one in which there is no consciousness of duality at all. The last of these experiences is not wholly different from the others. There is in it no experience of similarity in so far as this word is used to express identity in difference, or a relation between two. There can be no such relation unless there are two, and here there are not two. But it should be marked that this experience differs from the others, not in the element which has led us to declare two objects similar—the element which they have in common—but in that which has led us to declare them two and different. It is by adding to this last experience, so to speak, that we get the others. They contain it and more. Usage will not allow us to apply the term similarity in speaking of an experience in which two things are not distinguished, and this is proper enough ; but it should never be forgotten that this experience is at the bottom of all our experiences of similarity—is, so to speak, their common core. When, therefore, I said some pages back that all the kinds of sameness under discussion contain the idea of similarity, I was using the word in a certain broad sense to indicate that which is the ground of all our experiences of similarity, and is also found in the first kind of sameness on the list. I preferred to use there the word similarity, because it was easy to show that this notion is really contained in six of the seven uses of the word same, and it was convenient afterward to show the connection between the first kind of sameness and the notion of similarity.

And now it is not difficult to guess why we employ such expressions as we do to indicate strict identity. If I habitually use the proposition "x is y" to indicate a relation between two things having similar elements and yet regarded as distinct, and look upon the proposition as justified by the similar elements, observing that, these remaining unchanged, the dissimilar elements may be very variable without affecting the truth of the proposition, what more natural than that I should go on using the propositional form when the dissimilar elements have diminished to zero—when the proposition has become "x is x"? To be sure, no one can take such a proposition literally, any more than one can soberly believe that one divided by zero results in infinity. Such expressions have their use and value, but they must be properly understood. If one uses the expression "x is x" to emphasize the fact that one is not to pass from x to any y or z— that one is to rule out all distinction or sense of difference, the use cannot be harmful. And the use of the propositional form has this great convenience: it puts a period, so to speak, to one's thinking, and prevents one from casting about for a completion of the thought. If one merely say to me "x," I shall probably take it as a subject and busy myself to find a predicate. If he say "x is x," he says really no more than x, but he makes me fix my thoughts upon x alone.

SEC. 20. In the foregoing search for the element that the kinds of sameness have in common, I have had in mind chiefly the

samenesses of things immediately known. It is not necessary
to repeat the search in the field of the "external." We have but
the seven kinds of sameness, and whatever may be the things that
are the same in these several ways, the elements I have indicated must be present if our words are to be significant. But
one thing remains for me to do in this part of my monograph,
and that will not detain me long. I must distinguish between
sameness and identity, or rather point out to what kinds of
sameness this latter word is commonly applied.

The word is often used quite loosely, but where the attempt
is made to distinguish between identity and sameness in a looser
sense, and to use terms with some precision, the former word
serves to indicate sameness in which there is no consciousness
of duality, or in which the consciousness of duality has fallen into
the background and may easily be overlooked. Sameness of the
first kind, for example, is spoken of as identity. This is the only
kind of sameness in which there is no element of duality at all.
The use of the word identity is not, however, restricted to this.
Locke's inquiry concerning the identity of masses of inorganic
matter, of vegetables, of animals, and of persons, has to do with
sameness of the third kind on the list. In this kind of sameness
there is no clear consciousness that one is dealing with more
than one thing, and Locke's discussion is conducted throughout
as though one were not.

It may be objected that in certain other kinds there is often no
clear consciousness of duality, and yet one does not think of
using the term identity. This is quite true. The two kinds
mentioned have been thought worthy of special discussion by
logician and philosopher, and have been given a technical name.
The others have not. Still, although the word is not commonly
used in such cases, it would, I fancy, seem natural to use it in a
direct ratio to the degree in which the sense of duality falls into

the background. Dr. Johnson would probably have been willing to say that the stone he saw himself kick was identical with the one the existence of which he wanted to prove. Bishop Berkeley could have felt only disgust at such a use of the term. Scarcely anyone, I suppose, would regard himself as speaking strictly if he called the fourth kind of sameness identity. The co-existence of the two things compared would prevent their being confounded. Without, then, attempting to assign any very exact limits to the application of a somewhat loosely used word, I may repeat my former statement that men use the word identity to mark certain kinds of sameness in which there is little or no consciousness of duality, and they are not inclined to use it to mark samenesses in which things are recognized as similar but clearly distinct.

With this I end the first part of my discussion, and I confess I draw a long breath in doing so. When I sat down to write it was with the impression that I could say all that was necessary about the kinds of sameness in a much smaller number of pages; but finding it impossible to avoid misunderstandings without being more explicit and detailed, I have had to change my plan. Now, that I am through, I must confess to myself that most persons will find this hair-splitting anything but entertaining— which would be held by the inconsiderate to furnish a presumption against the truth it contains, if ancient adages go for anything. It should be remembered, however, that the old saw which puts truth in a well does not indicate that the well may not be a dry one. With this consolatory reflection I turn to the second part of my task.

PART II.

Those now who propose to hold mutual discussion must needs understand one another somewhat : for without this how can they have any mutual discussion? Each of their words then, must be familiar and have definite meaning, and not many meanings, but one only, and if it have more meanings than one, they must make it clear in which of these senses it is used.

Aristotle, Metaph., Book X, c. 5, § 3.

SECTION 21. When Heraclitus of Ephesus, moved thereto by his view of the constant flux of things, declared it impossible to enter the same river twice,[1] he evidently supposed that a river can be the same only in the first and strictest sense of the word. He denied, consequently, a right to use the word, as it constantly is used, to indicate that certain phenomena belong to a group or series, which, in its totality, is to us a single object. When we say that we have entered the same river twice we have no reference to the actual experiences of the two occasions considered merely as experiences. Of course, these are not the same, as each is itself, and they may even be somewhat dissimilar. Nor have we reference to the separate particles of which the body of water is composed. We all admit that the water in a river changes, and yet we never think of saying that the river is no longer the same. The two kinds of sameness are quite distinct, yet both are legitimate; and both were as familiar to the ancient Greek as to the modern American. Socrates was considered Socrates from boyhood through youth to manhood. The Ilissus was the Ilissus whether swollen or shrunken. The philosopher's difficulty with the river did not arise out of

[1] Aristotle, Metaph., Bk. III, c. 5, § 7.

the fact that this kind of sameness was not perfectly well recognized in language and in common thought. It arose out of the fact that the beginnings of reflection make many things seem strange which before passed unnoticed, and sometimes lead to assertion and denial evidently contrary to experience and common sense. The unreflective man calls the river the same on two successive days, but he has no clear notion of what the word implies. In a loose way he opposes "same" to "different." Heraclitus saw that the water in a river is constantly changing. He who enters twice does not enter precisely the same body of water. What more natural, and what more fallacious, than to assert that he does not twice enter the same river?

SEC. 22. And well might Cratylus hold his peace and move his finger[1] when he had capped the climax with the statement that the same river could not be entered once. Heraclitus had merely denied sameness of the third kind to be sameness, since it implies duality. Cratylus, surprised by a discovery of duality where he had not before suspected it, will not allow the term where there is no duality whatever. It is not surprising that he came at last to be "of opinion that one ought to speak of nothing." Upon such a basis speech loses its significance.

SEC. 23. The Parmenidean argument for the eternity of Being[2] rests partly upon a confusion of the first kind of sameness with the fourth. Being has had no origin, for from what could it have been derived? Not from the non-existent, for this has no existence: and not from the existent, for it is itself the existent. The quibble about the non-existent we need not consider, though it is seriously repeated by more than one writer of our time. The last part of the argument, "not from the existent, for it is itself the existent," draws its whole force from the assumption

---

[1] Aristotle, Metaph. III, c. 5, § 7.
[2] Ueberweg. Hist. of Philos., Vol. I, § 19. N. Y., 1877, p. 57.

that "it" is "the existent" as a thing is itself, or in the first sense of the word same. But if this be the case, the argument is a mere farce, an argument only in words. The phrase, "derived from the existent," means nothing at all unless it means that the existent in question is before the thing derived. To say it *is* the thing derived, is to reduce the words to nothing. If it mean anything to speak of the existent as derived from the existent, it is because each of these is *an* existent—that is, a thing belonging to a class and distinguished from other members of this class by some difference. In this case the difference is that of before and after. An existent derived from an existent is the same with it only as things of a class are the same. If we choose to eliminate all differences and speak of "*the* existent" we may do so; but then it is inadmissible to raise questions about its derivation, and bring in those very time distinctions between different "existents" which we are supposing absent.

SEC. 24. The nihilistic doctrine of Gorgias of Leontini,[1] who taught that nothing exists, that if it did exist it could not be known, and that if it did exist and could be known the knowledge of it could not be communicated by one mind to another, is founded in part upon such bad reasoning that it is rather surprising that Gorgias should have been guilty of it. That part of it, however, which has to do with the communicability of knowledge is rather better than the rest, and indicates some progress in reflection. A sign, he says, differs from the thing it signifies. How can one communicate the notion of color by words, since the ear hears sounds and not colors? Besides, how can the same idea be in two different persons? This reasoning would seem at least plausible, I think, to many minds at the present day. It is evidently the offspring of a confusion of samenesses. A sign dif-

---

[1] Ueberweg. Hist. of Philos., Vol. I, § 29. p. 77.

fers, it is true, from the thing signified. The word blue heard by the ear is not like the color blue seen or imagined. But if any one pronounce the word, and ask me if I am thinking of the color he has mentioned, I say yes. The sound is not like the color, but it is its representative, and one of the proper uses of the word same (the fifth) indicates just this relation between representative and thing represented. Any attempt to discredit communication of knowledge on the ground that one cannot speak colors, and that, therefore, one man is speaking one thing and the other thinking another, goes on the supposition that what is said and what is thought must be the same in sense first (strict identity) or in sense fourth (must be a thing of the same kind). And as to the existence of the same thing in two minds; here Gorgias has evidently discovered with some surprise that sameness in sense sixth differs from sameness in sense first, and has felt impelled to deny it the name altogether. He has perceived a duality where most men have not noticed it; and, instead of observing that there are samenesses and samenesses, and that the communication of knowledge is concerned with the sixth kind in this connection, and not with the first, he has denied the communication of knowledge. Had he found it necessary to carry out his theoretic premises to practical conclusions he would have stopped talking, which he did not; though presumably the irrepressible didactic instinct would have led him, spite of consistency, to imitate Cratylus in moving his finger.

Sec. 25. The reasoning in the Platonic Dialogues is very frequently not above suspicion; but it is not easy to find anywhere such a nest of paralogisms as we have in the Parmenides. How far Plato was in earnest in all this quibbling, and what was his aim, I will not pretend to say. He has, however, very well illustrated the possibilities of equivocation in juggling with samenesses, and

I shall quote a bit of the argument concerning the one and the many to show how readily this is done. Almost any part of the dialogue would do, but I choose the first bout between Parmenides and Aristoteles. I take Professor Jowett's version:[1]

Parmenides proceeded: If one is, he said, the one cannot be many?

Impossible.

Then the one cannot have parts, and cannot be a whole?

How is that?

Why, the part would surely be the part of a whole?

Yes.

And that of which no part is wanting, would be a whole?

Certainly.

Then, in either case, one would be made up of parts; both as being a whole, and also as having parts?

Certainly.

And in either case, the one would be many, and not one?

True.

But, surely, one ought to be not many, but one?

Surely.

Then, if one is to remain one, it will not be a whole, and will not have parts?

No.

And if one has no parts, it will have neither beginning, middle, nor end; for these would be parts of one?

Right.

But then, again, a beginning and an end are the limits of everything?

Certainly.

Then the one, neither having beginning nor end, is unlimited?

Yes, unlimited.

[1] The Dialogues of Plato. N. Y., 1878. Vol. III, p. 255.

And therefore formless, as not being able to partake either of round or straight.

How is that?

Why, the round is that of which all the extreme points are equidistant from the centre?

Yes.

And the straight is that of which the middle intercepts the extremes?

True.

Then the one would have parts, and would be many, whether it partook of a straight or of a round form?

Assuredly.

But having no parts, one will be neither straight nor round?

Right.

Then, being of such a nature, one cannot be in any place, for it cannot be either in another or in itself.

How is that?

Because, if one be in another, it will be encircled in that other in which it is contained, and will touch it in many places; but that which is one and indivisible, and does not partake of a circular nature, cannot be touched by a circle in many places.

Certainly not.

And one being in itself, will also contain itself, and cannot be other than one, if in itself; for nothing can be in anything which does not contain it.

Impossible.

But then, is not that which contains other than that which is contained? for the same whole cannot at once be affected actively and passively; and one will thus be no longer one, but two?

True.

Then one cannot be anywhere, either in itself or in another?

No.

Further consider, whether that which is of such a nature can have either rest or motion.

Why not?

Why, because motion is either motion in place or change in self; these are the only kinds of motion.

Yes.

And the one, when changed in itself, cannot possibly be any longer one.

It cannot.

And therefore cannot experience this sort of motion?

Clearly not.

Can the motion of one, then, be in place?

Perhaps.

But if one moved in place, must it not either move round and round in the same place, or from one place to another?

Certainly.

And that which moves round and round in the same place, must go round upon a centre; and that which goes round upon a centre must have other parts which move around the centre; but that which has no centre and no parts cannot possibly be carried round upon a centre?

Impossible.

But perhaps the motion of the one consists in going from one place to another?

Perhaps so, if it moves at all.

And have we not already shown that one can not be in anything?

Yes.

And still greater is the impossibility of one coming into being in anything?

I do not see how that is.

Why, because anything which comes into being in anything,

cannot as yet be in that other thing while still coming into being, nor remain entirely out of it, if already coming into being in it.

Certainly.

And therefore whatever comes into being in another must have parts, and the one part may be in that other, and the other part out of it; but that which has no parts cannot possibly be at the same time a whole, which is either within or without anything.

True.

And how can that which has neither parts, nor a whole, come into being anywhere either as a part or a whole? Is not that a still greater impossibility?

Clearly.

Then one does not change by a change of place, whether by going somewhere and coming into being in something; or again, by going round in the same place; or again, by change in itself?

True.

The one, then, is incapable of any kind of motion?

Incapable.

But neither can the one exist in anything, as we affirm?

Yes, that is affirmed by us.

Then it is never in the same?

Why not?

Because being in the same is being in something which is the same.

Certainly.

But it cannot be in itself, and cannot be in other?

True.

Then one is never the same?[1]

It would seem not.

---

[1] The text of Stallbaum (1848) does not harmonize with this. The version I quote leaves out ἐν, and reads τὸ αὐτό in the nominative.

And that which is never in the same has no rest, and stands not still?

It cannot stand still.

One, then, as would seem, is neither standing still nor in motion?

Clearly not.

Neither will one be the same with itself or other; nor again, other than itself, or other.

How is that?

If other than itself it would be other than one, and would not be one.

True.

And if the same with other, it would be that other, and not itself; so that upon this supposition, too, it would not have the nature of one, but would be other than one?

It would.

Then it will not be the same with other, or other than itself?

It will not.

Neither will one be other than other, while it remains one; for not the one, but only the other, can be other of other, and nothing else.

True.

Then not by virtue of being one, will one be other?

Certainly not.

But if not by virtue of being one, not by virtue of being itself; and if not by virtue of being itself, not itself, and itself not being other at all, will not be other of anything?

Right.

Neither will one be the same with itself.

Why not?

Because the nature of the one is surely not the nature of the same.

Why is that?

Because when a thing becomes the same with anything, it does not necessarily become one.

Why not?

That which becomes the same with the many necessarily becomes many and not one.

True.

And yet, if there were no difference between the one and the same, when a thing became the same, it would always become one; and when it became one, the same.

Certainly.

And, therefore, if one be the same with one, it is not one with one, and will therefore be one and also not one.

But that is surely impossible.

And therefore the one can neither be other of other, nor the same with one.

Impossible.

And thus one is neither the same, nor other, in relation to itself or other?

No.

Neither will one be like or unlike itself or other.

Why not?

Because likeness is sameness of affections.

Yes.

And sameness has been shown to be a nature distinct from oneness?

That has been shown.

But if one had any other affection than that of being one, it would be affected in such a way as to be more than one; and that is impossible.

True.

Then one can never have the same affections either as another or as itself?

Clearly not.

Then it cannot be like other, or like itself.

No.

Nor can it be affected so as to be other, for then it would be affected in such a way as to be more than one.

It would.

That which is affected in a manner other than itself or other, will be unlike itself or other, if sameness of affections is likeness.

True.

But the one, as appears, never having affections other than its own, is never unlike itself or other?

Never.

Then the one is never either like or unlike itself or other?

Plainly not.

In reading this extract one cannot but admire the courtesy or wonder at the simplicity of Aristoteles. He always answers just as he should to keep the ball rolling; and he is in no wise compelled to do this under the circumstances, for the argument is loose in the extreme. Briefly stated, the reasoning is as follows:

One cannot be a whole, and cannot have parts, for then it would not be one, but many. But if it has no parts it has no beginning, middle, or end, and is formless. It is then in no place, for it cannot be in itself, since the container must be different from the thing contained; nor can it be in other, for it would have to be encircled by that other, and touched in many parts, which is impossible. It follows that it can neither be at rest nor in motion. Not in motion; for it cannot have change in itself, or it would no longer be one; nor can it have motion in place, whether circular motion upon a centre or motion from place to place; the former for the reason that circular motion implies a centre and parts around the centre; and the latter because one is in no place: and as to coming into being in anything, which may be regarded as a kind of motion, while doing this it would have to be part in and part not in, which is impossible. It cannot be at rest, for one is never in the same; to be in the same, is to be in something which is the same, and one cannot be in anything. Nor, farther, can one be the same with itself or other, nor other than itself or other. If other than itself it would not be one; and if the same with other it would be that other, and not itself. On the other hand only other can be the other of other, and not one; and the one cannot be the same with itself, for the nature of the one is not the nature of the same, since that which becomes the same with the many does not become one. Finally, one cannot be like or unlike itself or other, for likeness is sameness of affections, and sameness is not oneness; one must, however, have no affection except oneness, or it becomes more than one. It cannot, then, have the same affections as itself or other. As, for the same reason, it cannot have other affections than itself or other, it cannot be unlike.

We have here one chief error, which runs through almost the whole of the argument—is, indeed, the "Kern" of the "Pudel"— and several subsidiary errors of different kinds. Some of these last are very readily discovered, as that about the coming into being in a thing. With these, however, I am not concerned. I merely remark *en passant* that they may all be cleared up with a little care and accuracy, and I turn to the main error, which consists in a constant confusion of two kinds of sameness. The fact is that Parmenides is always passing from "the one," or one in the abstract, mere oneness, to "a one," or one object. These are no more identical in the strict sense than "manhood" and "a man," and in overlooking their difference he is simply confounding the first and the fourth kinds of sameness. "The one" cannot have parts, for the good reason that it is a quality taken by itself, and not a thing, which is thought as a bundle of qualities. "A one," on the other hand, may have parts, and each of these parts may be "a one" too. "A one" by no means consists of a single element, oneness, but of this element combined with others; and each such group may be distinguished from each other such group, and all be recognized as similar, or the same in a true sense of the word. The question whether one can be in a place, too, evidently has to do, not with "the one," but "a one," for spacial or temporal differences are invidualizing, and distinguish a thing from another thing of the same kind. To ask whether "the one" may or may not be in a place is inadmissible.

The same error is at the bottom of the argument about the one's being in motion or at rest. The question has no significance except in reference to "a one." If we speak of "the one" as in motion, we at once put this abstract element in such a relation to other elements that we have no longer "the one" but "a one." "The one" cannot have change in itself and remain "the one," but "a one" may change a good deal and still be "a one." And without admitting the justice of the argument, that what has no parts cannot be in anything, the proof of the impossibility of motion in space may be condemned merely upon the ground that it is only "the one" which cannot have parts, while it is only "a one" which is concerned in the problem of motion. The same may be said for the argument against the one's coming into being in anything. It is only "a one" which can be thought as coming into being in a thing, and "a one" may have parts. As for the impossibility of the one's being at rest, on the ground that to be at rest, a thing must be in the same, and one cannot be in anything—this is a repetition of the former error. "A one" may be in something, as has been pointed out, even on the basis established at the outset, and it is with this, and not with "the one," that we are concerned in the problem of rest and motion.

The rest of the argument is based upon errors of a different kind, and in it one may keep to "the one" throughout, if one choose. There is, of course, no reason to think that the speaker did this. He probably here, as before, carried over to "a one," one thought as an individual thing, distinctions drawn in view of "the one," one viewed in the abstract. As some of the statements made may be true or false as one is taken in this sense or that; and particularly as the antinomy rests upon a misconception as to the nature of sameness, I will continue the analysis. What is to be proved is, first, that one cannot be the same with itself or other, or other than itself or other ; and second, that it cannot be like or unlike itself or other. The position that the one, if other than itself, would not be one, and if the same with other, would be that other, is somewhat ambiguous. If "a one" is in question, it may undoubtedly be "a one" and yet be other than any particular one; and it may be the same with other—another one—without ceasing to be one, if by same we mean similar. The play upon words in "other of other" it is not necessary to consider. The conclusion that one cannot be the same with itself is based upon the supposition that sameness is a quality superadded to the other qualities of a thing; but in its first sense the word does not even serve to indicate a relation ; it is merely used to point out the absence of duality. Both "a one" and "the one" may be the same with themselves perfectly well, and in saying so we do not in thought endow them with any quality not already possessed. This last error serves also as a basis to the second paradoxical position, that one cannot be like or unlike itself or other. It assumes likeness and unlikeness to be qualities added to the other qualities of things which are like or unlike.

A possible objection to my use of the term "a one" I must forestall before passing on. I have used this as synonymous with "one object." One horse is one object, and so is one part of a horse. It may be said, however, that "a one" may also be used to signify a single occurrence of oneness, as distinguished from another occurrence of oneness. That any element of consciousness may be distinguished from any similar element merely by spatial or temporal differences I have argued in the first part of my monograph. Why may not then "a one" mean the oneness of this one horse, or the oneness of this part of the horse? And if it may, can "a one" of this kind have parts any more than "the one?"

I answer, it cannot; for it is then only a particular occurrence of the quality (if I may so use the word) of oneness. But, then, if we so understand the term, the argument loses all significance. We cannot call "a one" of this kind a container or a thing contained, or talk of it as encircled by anything. We do not even try to imagine it as moving on its centre, or passing from place to place, or coming into being in anything, or being at rest in anything. Such language we use only in speaking of things. It seems to me plain that the speaker is thinking of one as a thing, and it is this that gives its charm to the bundle of paradoxes. The Eleatic "one" was always a thing and not mere unity or an occurrence of unity. My criticism of the reasoning is, I think, just. And whether Plato is responsible for the Parmenides or not, we must agree that such a confusion of "the one" and "a one" (as an object) would not be foreign to his modes of thought. His world of Ideas is peopled with "the"'s turned into "a"'s, a fact which his acute pupil Aristotle was not slow to discover.[1]

[1] Metaph. XII, c. 4.

Sec. 26. Aristotle has again and again discussed with his usual keenness the kinds of sameness. He saw well enough that the word is ambiguous, and may with equal right be employed in speaking of experiences which do or do not contain an element of duality. He has pointed out that the law of non-contradiction has to do with sameness of the first kind, and not with the others.[1] His question as to "Socrates" and "Socrates sitting," his treatment of "Coriscus" and "the musical Coriscus," his statement that the white and the musical are the same when they are accidents in the same subject,[2] show that he clearly understood the significance of sameness in sense third. He gives us sense fourth when he says that things may be called the same when they belong to the same species or genus.[3] In his polemic against the Protagorean doctrine of relativity,[4] senses sixth and seventh come to the surface, though they are not very clearly or exhaustively discussed. The fallacy in the apparent possibility of attributing contradictory predicates to the same subject, from the fact that the same wine may appear sweet to one taster and not sweet to another, or at one time sweet and at another not sweet to the one palate, is laid bare in the distinction between kinds of sameness. Aristotle distinguishes between the wine itself and the sensations it produces in different persons, and he recognizes the fact that one man's perception of the "same" wine need not be wholly like that of another. But this does not imply any violation of the law of non-contradiction, for each sensation is just what it is at any instant; and the statement that the same wine is sweet and not sweet at the one moment amounts only to saying that the one object can cause dissimilar sensations in two minds at one moment. As much may be said

[1] Metaph. III, c. 5, § 10; c. 6, § 3.
[2] Ibid. III, c. 2, § 6; IV, c. 6, § 1, and c. 9, § 1.
[3] Ibid. IV, c. 9, § 1, and c. 6.
[4] Ibid. III, c. 5, § 10; X, c. 6, § 6.

for the non-simultaneous sensations of the one man. Sensations differing in time are two, and may differ without violating any law. In marking the fact that when we say two men perceive the same thing we do not mean that the immediate object of knowledge is in the two cases strictly one, but merely that these two objects are related in a peculiar way, Aristotle draws the line between sameness in sense first and in sense sixth. As to sense seventh. He distinguishes between the apparent and the real, and yet goes on speaking, quite in modern fashion, as though one thing could serve for both. He points out, à propos of pressing upon the eyeball and doubling the visual image, that there is a distinction between the apparent and the real, and then closes the paragraph with the remark that " to those persons who do not move their organ of vision that which is one appears one."[1] This language would certainly seem to indicate that that which is appears—or that they are the same in some strict sense of the word. The sentence reads much in the style of Mr. Spencer or Sir William Hamilton.

It appears, then, that Aristotle recognized a sameness in which there is no sense of duality, and samenesses in which two things are called the same and yet distinguished as two. Our way of expressing strict identity, however, a way which, as I have shown, does not properly express it all—seems to have misled him into finding a sort of quasi duality even here, where he knows it to be really absent. In a chapter[2] devoted to sameness and diversity, he closes his list of samenesses with the remark : " It is plain that sameness is a oneness either of two or more things with reference to their essence, or of one thing treated as two ; as when you say a thing is the same with itself, for then you do treat it as two." We do employ two words, undoubtedly ; but if we are really thinking a thing as itself, we are not making it

---

[1] Metaph. X, c. 6, § 2.   [2] Ibid. IV, c. 9.

dual in any sense whatever. The quotation smacks just a little of Cratylus.

SEC. 27. The sceptical arguments of Pyrrho are excellent instances of a confusion of samenesses. The argument, for example, that since an apple seen by the eye as yellow seems to the taste sweet, and to the smell as fragrant, " that which is seen is just as likely to be something else as the reality ;"[1] this argu ment gains what little plausibility it may have from the assump- tion that an object seen and an object tasted are (or ought to be) the same in sense first instead of sense third.

And the complaints, that things believed to be large, some. times, as when at a distance, appear small ; that things which we believe to be straight, sometimes seem bent ; that the sun has one appearance in the morning, and another at noon ;[2] these, and all others like them, assume that an object seen near at hand and then seen at a distance, a stick seen as straight and then seen as crooked, the sun on the horizon and the sun at the zenith, are in each case one strictly, and not merely one as each element in a complex of experiences is one with each other element, when any one may represent the whole. The conclusion that, since it is not possible to view things without reference to " place and position," their true nature cannot be known,[3] is founded upon this error.

This becomes clear when one asks, what is it, after all, the nature of which is so in doubt? Is it a stick? the sun ? These words are ambiguous. Two consecutive experiences of the same stick—as we ordinarily use this word in speaking of sticks—are not strictly identical, and need not be alike. The stick seen on two occasions is not the same stick in sense I. If I limit the meaning of the words "the stick" to one of these expe-

[1] Diogenes Laërtius. IX, 9.
[2] *Ibid.* loc. cit.
[3] *Ibid.* loc. cit.

riences, then the true nature of the stick is just what is experienced on that occasion. What is experienced on the second occasion is another stick, and its true nature is also just what it seems to be. If, however, by "the stick" I do not mean only the experience of one moment, but a series of experiences differing more or less from one another, then I am under no necessity to select one of them as the true nature of the stick, for its true nature is nothing more nor less than the whole group of experiences. If I try to discover or to invent some new experience which I may call the true nature of the group, I am simply adding to it in thought another experience which takes its place among those the group already contains. I am playing with the word nature. This last experience could not be more important than those among which it is placed, and it could not stand for any one of them in any other way than each of them could stand for it. Should it be objected that by "the stick" one does not mean either a single experience of the stick or the sum total of the group of experiences, but a something distinct from all these and inferred through them, I answer, that in this case the argument from the variability of experiences is not to the point. Such a "stick" as this would be the same with either of those just discussed only in the seventh sense of the word, and its nature would be the same with their nature only in that sense too. An experience of the stick out of "place and position," if that were conceivable, would not give us this "stick," for such an expe- rience would still be an experience. It must never be forgotten that this "external" stick is quite distinct from any or all experiences, and could not be given in experiences of any kind. It can only be inferred. If an unvarying series of experiences is good ground for inferring an unvarying "external" stick, similar to what is experienced, one would suppose a varying series of experiences would furnish a basis for inference of a varying

" external" stick, in its successive phases like what is experienced. Unless some reason is given for a discrimination in favor of the unvarying series, the argument from variation does not affect the " external" stick at all.

It is evident, however, that in this particular argument, at least, the "external" is not in Pyrrho's mind at all. What perplexes him is, that what he is accustomed to call a straight stick sometimes looks crooked. On reflection he discovers that he calls it straight only because it seems straight on some occasions ; and if it may at one time seem straight and at another seem crooked, which is it in reality ? The question is a very natural one. The unreflective do not ask it, because they assume that one of the experiences is to be taken as expressing the true nature of the object and the other relegated to the sphere of more or less deceptive appearance. The man who has begun to reflect does ask it, because he sees that the assumed true nature is an appearance too, and it naturally occurs to him that it also may be deceptive. If he reflected more, he would see that he is partly right and partly wrong. We do not regard as equally important every element in the group of experiences which we call an object. Certain elements, notably the tactual qualities and those visual experiences which give us the best opportunity of inferring the tactual qualities, stand in the foreground when we speak of the object. We name the object according to these. In saying "a straight stick" we have prominently in mind certain tactual experiences, and certain visual experiences which normally are connected with these and give us the right to infer them. We call any appearance delusive which leads us to infer tactual experiences, and visual experiences of a kind regarded as best representative of these tactual experiences, when such cannot be actually experienced. Certain elements in the total group, which is to us an experienced object, may then properly be regarded as in a sense the true nature of the object, they are the most important part, and the part to which other elements are referred. These elements may justly be regarded as delusive when they mislead us in our inferences as to the important elements. So far the common man is right. And as no element is delusive in itself, but only in so far as it refers the mind to something else, and to the wrong something else, those elements which are ultimate and not used as signs of others, cannot be delusive. In raising this question with regard to them Pyrrho is wrong. These elements may, to be sure, be used as signs or indications of any other elements in the group, and in their turn made stepping stones; but this is not commonly done, and language and common thought rarely mark logical possibilities. The language in use fairly expresses the attitude of the average man towards the elements in his thought.

On the other hand, the unreflective man speaks as if the less important, or perhaps I had better say less prominent, experiences were not a part of the object as he knows it. He seems to regard the whole object as actually present, when a single experience only is present. In putting all experiences on the same plane, so to speak, the Pyrrhonist makes a genuine advance. Wherein he errs is this: He sees that a stick seen near at hand is as much an experience or appearance as a stick seen at a distance, and that one of these phenomena does not differ in kind from the other; he sees also that to assume that one is the real stick and the other is not, seems to go upon the assumption that they differ in kind; he is consequently unwilling to call any one of his experiences the real stick, and yet he insists upon looking for a real stick, which may be expressed in a single experience. It never seems to occur to him that the real stick may be the name of the whole series of experiences in their appropriate relations. He wishes a sameness in the strict sense, with no element of duality. The stick seen straight in the air, and seen bent in the water, is the same stick in sense third. It takes both of these experiences to express the true nature of this stick. No one experience could serve. It is the battle between stick as a single experience, and stick as a group of experiences, that leads to all the confusion.

I have given as much space to Pyrrho as I care to, and I will not delay over him and his successors. These furnish good material to one fond of analysis. There is, however, a great deal of repetition among the sceptics. They occupy themselves chiefly either in confounding the first kind of sameness with the third, as in the preceding ; or in confounding the first kind with the sixth, as in the argument for uncertainty drawn from the varying guise under which the same object appears to different persons. The ambiguity of the word same, as here used, is apparent, and it is in this ambiguity that they become entangled.

SEC. 28. Into the labyrinths of the scholastic philosophy I hesitate to enter, and yet I could hardly be excused for passing on to the moderns without at least a reference to the great dispute over Universals—a dispute which is, at bottom, a quarrel concerning samenesses. I shall speak of it very briefly.

The object of the general term or class name is in question. Plato, distinguishing between the universal and the individual, between man and men, thought it necessary, according to Aristotle, who has not, I think, done him injustice, to assume an object for the universal outside of and apart from all the individuals forming a class. The Idea is a real thing, *the* real thing in which the individuals participate, or of which they are copies ; but it is not itself to be found in any or all of them, except, so to speak, in a figurative or metaphorical way. Aristotle, finding no reason to assume a new individual, for so he regarded the Platonic Idea, placed the universal *in* the individuals composing the class. Certain of the schoolmen, emphasizing the distinction between real things and mental representations, maintained that only individuals have real existence, and asserted either that universals exist merely as peculiar combinations of mental elements which serve to think the objects forming a class, or that the universal is the word, which may be applied indifferently to many individuals of one kind. In these views we have the *universalia ante rem*, the *universalia in re*, and the *universalia post rem ;* or extreme Realism, moderate Realism, and Nominalism in its two forms.

The examination into the respective merits of the positions which have been taken with regard to universals will be facilitated by distinguishing carefully between the different spheres of being ; that is, between things immediately known and "real" things mediately known, as also between things contained in one consciousness and those contained in another. It is plainly important not to confound these classes with each other.

Let us take, first, a number of resembling objects in a single consciousness. I have already pointed out that when we say several such objects are the same we do not at all mean to deny that they are distinct objects. We merely wish to indicate that each possesses certain elements which, taken by themselves, and after making abstraction from all other elements, render impossible any distinction between different objects. We distinguish two objects as two through some difference, even if it be only local or temporal. Redness combined with x and redness combined with y are recognized as two occurrences of redness, but this only on account of x and y. Redness perceived to-day and redness perceived yesterday are two occurrences of redness, marked as such by the "to-day" and the "yesterday." Redness considered simply contains nothing which will allow of such distinctions. This does not imply at all that redness considered simply is *an occurrence of redness*—that since we have not two or more occurrence of the quality we have a single occurrence of it, an individual. We have not, if we have really abstracted from all save the redness, any "occurrence" or "occurrences" at all, for these imply just the elements of difference which we are endeavoring to eliminate. An "occurrence" of redness means redness with a difference which will mark it out from other redness, from another "occurrence." If, then, one gives to twenty individuals a common name to indicate that they resemble each other, or are in some sense the same, he should keep clearly in mind just what this means. It means that along with various differing elements each contains the element x. He should remember that each individual is the same with each other individual only in this sense, sense fourth. When he proposes to separate the x from the other elements, and consider it separately, he should be most careful to see that he is really taking it separately, and not allowing shreds of foreign matter to hang to it and give rise to difficulties and perplexities. He should not overlook the fact that there is a fallacy in the very question, Whether the x in one individual is identical (the same in sense first) with the x in any other individual? If these two x's are distinguishable as in two individuals, one is not considering x merely, but x with other elements. The separation of the x element from the other elements in the objects is here not complete, or one would be considering not "an x" or "x's," but x. Any one who sees this must see that he who asks such a question is retaining a duality, and then trying to get out of it an identity with no element of duality. He is "milking the he-goat." He is trying to reduce sameness in sense fourth to sameness in sense first.

Twenty objects immediately known must not be confounded with twenty "real" things not immediately known, and of which the objects are supposed to be representatives. These two classes are the same with each other only in sense seventh. I have discussed in detail in the first part of my monograph the samenesses of "real" things, and it is not necessary to repeat what I have said. It is enough to state that it was there made evident that when we speak of a number of similar "real" things as the same, we use the word in sense fourth, and have in mind just the elements which are present when we speak of several similar immediate objects of knowledge as the same. We are merely carrying over to a set of imagined duplicates a distinction which we observe in objects recognized as within consciousness. When, therefore, we give twenty "real" things a common name, and form them into a class, because they are alike, we mean that along with various other "real" elements, each of these objects contains the "real" element x. The word same means to us just what it does when we speak of twenty similar immediate objects as the same. We have changed only the objects ; we have not changed the sameness and all that depends upon it. Two such objects are the same in sense fourth, and never in sense first. If they could be the same in sense first, they would not be two. When a man undertakes to separate in thought the "real" x element from the other "real" elements in two or more such objects, he should be careful, as in the case of immediate objects, to make a complete separation and not a partial one. He should see here, too, that the question whether the x in one object and the x in another are strictly identical, is a foolish one. "This x" and "that x" are not strictly identical, or they would not be "this x" and "that x." Remove completely the "this" and the "that" and all other differing elements—leave, that is, only x, and the possibility of any such question simply disappears. If there still seem to any one ground for a question in the premises, it is evidence that he is not considering merely x. He is trying to keep two things two, and yet make them one.

Twenty objects in one consciousness must not be confounded with twenty objects in another. When we speak of two men as seeing the same thing, we do not mean that the object in one mind is the same with the object in the other in sense first, but in sense sixth. This does not prevent them from being two. A single object in one mind may be the same with itself in sense first. A number of similar objects in one mind may be the same in sense fourth. Two objects or two classes of objects in different minds may be the same in sense sixth. One may, to be sure, think of twenty objects in one mind, and of the same (sense sixth) twenty objects in another mind as forty objects. Philosophical reflection naturally leads to this. I am inducing a reader to do it when I tell him that an object in one mind and the same object in another are two objects. But in doing this, one must bear in mind the fact that the forty objects belong to two quite distinct classes, and that common language would not reckon them as forty, but as twenty. In this there is, of course, a pitfall for the unwary.

Now, when Plato looked for the object of the general name, for the x contained in a class of similar objects, what did he do? He created a new object distinct from and apart from all the others. He is very vague in his statements, and he was probably quite as vague in his thought; but I cannot see how anyone familiar with the Phaedrus, the Republic, the Timaeus, the Symposium and the Parmenides, and familiar with Plato's concrete way of thinking in images, can avoid coming to the conclusion that the Idea was to him predominantly an object, an individual —a vague and inconsistent object, if you please, but still an object. But *an* x is in no sense a universal. It is the same with other x's only in sense fourth; that is, it is like them. The x that they have in common must be x considered simply, not x considered as here or there, in this place or in that. All such differences must be eliminated if one is to get not an individual, but a universal. If the Idea may be considered as *apart* from objects, it is an object in so far not essentially differing from the others. Again, the Platonic Idea is an object, but not to be put upon the same plane with other objects. They suffer change, while it is immutable; they are perceivable by the senses, and it is not. The objects of sense and the Idea are in different worlds; and though we cannot accuse Plato of drawing the distinctions of the modern hypothetical realist, he has certainly given us a suggestive parallel to the Lockian ideas and "real" things. The trouble has arisen out of his difficulty in keeping an abstraction abstract; he has turned it into a concrete, and, finding in the world of sense no place for this concrete, this new individual, he has given it a world of its own. Whatever this object in this world apart may be, it is certainly not what is common to twenty individuals in the world of sensible things.

Aristotle, seeing this difficulty, placed the idea *in* the objects forming the class. It may be objected that putting x *in* a place individualizes it as much as putting it *out of* a place. This is quite true if the "in" is taken locally—taken as it is when we speak of a man as being in one room rather than another. The x in one object is not identically the x in another object. We do not get the universal, x in the abstract, until we lose the distinctions "in the one object," and "in the other object." Two x's cannot be the same in sense first, from the mere fact that they are two; an x in one place and an x in another place are always two. If, however, by the statement that the universal is in the objects, one mean merely that the universal is that element x, which, combined with certain elements, forms a total which is known as this object, and combined with certain others forms a total which is known as that, but taken by itself contains no distinction of this and that ; if this is all that is meant by the "in," there is no objection to the use of the statement, and it is strictly true. The x element is a part of each of the objects, but, until some addition is made to it, it is not "the x in this object " or "the x in that object"; it is what they have in common. The "in common" means just this.

The Nominalistic doctrine that only individuals have real existence, and that the universal, whatever it may be, is to be sought in the mind, distinguishes between the spheres of being and denies to one what it allows to another. Of the extreme nominalistic position, that the only true universal is the word, which may be applied indifferently to several distinct objects, I shall not here speak. I have discussed this wholly untenable view elsewhere.[1] But the more reasonable Nominalism, the conceptualistic, is worthy of examination here. In so far as it holds that the mind can form a concept, which shall consist of the element or elements several objects have in common, we have no quarrel with it. Here we find a true universal, obtained by discarding differences which distinguish objects from one another. We obtain by this that mental core common to several similar mental objects. If, however, we distinguish between mental objects and "real" things corresponding to them, we have evidently two distinct fields to consider. When we say a number of objects in consciousness are alike, we are simply pointing out the fact that they contain a universal element as well as individual differences. Can we say that a number of "real" objects are alike? If so, what do we mean in saying it? If

[1] See my "Conception of the Infinite," Cb. VI (J. B. Lippincott Co., Philadelphia). It is but fair to state that my criticism of Realism in this volume is directed against the "*ante rem*" Realism. I did not have the Moderate Realism in mind, and what I said will not apply to it.

there is nothing to prevent us from calling them individuals, there would seem to be nothing to prevent us from affirming that they are "really" alike. Does likeness ever mean anything except sameness in difference? Is not, then, the element in which several objects resemble each other a universal element, whether the objects be mental or "real?" What else does universal mean? The excuse for speaking ceases when language ceases to be significant. One does not in the least explain the similarity, or sameness in the fourth sense, of a number of "real" objects, by assuming a universal in a quite different world—one which could not possibly exist in the world of the objects. This solution of the problem is Platonic. The element which twenty real objects have in common must be a "real" element, or it cannot be a constituent part of each object. If it is not a constituent part of each object, it is absurd to speak of the objects as having it in common. If they have nothing in common, it is absurd to say that they are alike. Twenty similar objects must have a universal element, to whatever sphere of being they belong; and this element must belong to the same sphere as the objects. A mental universal is the same with a "real" universal only in sense seventh, and it can furnish no explanation of the likeness of "real" things.

In the light of the foregoing analysis a goodly number of the scholastic arguments regarding universals are easily seen to contain errors. The Anselmic view of genera and species as universal substances,[1] for instance, makes an abstraction a thing and distinguishes it from other things. It fails to keep it abstract. The doctrine attributed to William of Champeaux, by Abelard, that universals are essentially and wholly present in each of their individuals, in which latter there is no diversity of essence, but only variety through accidents,[2] is tenable or not

---

[1] Hauréau. *Philos. Scholastique.* Paris, 1872. I, p. 281.
[2] *Historia Calamitatum*, quoted by Hauréau. I, p. 324.

according to the sense in which the words are taken. The word "wholly" is an awkward one, and would incline one to the view that William regarded the universal as a thing, a concrete, which may be in this place or that. If this were his opinion, and it is perhaps more reasonable to believe that it was, the objection of Abelard, that this would necessitate the same thing's being in different places at the same time, would hold good. If the essence of humanity be wholly in Socrates, it must be where Socrates is. It cannot, then, be somewhere else in Plato. Manifestly humanity, so regarded, is not a universal at all. It is "this humanity" or "that humanity," *i. e.*, this or that occurrence of humanity; and two occurrences of a quality or group of qualities are two individuals. The word "in" I have shown to be ambiguous. Any element, regarded as, in one sense, *in* an individual, retains the local flavor which makes universality impossible. But if William meant nothing more by his statement than that the element common to the individuals is a constituent part of each, and that there is in it no distinction which will allow us to put it part here and part there, the polemic of Abelard is not justifiable. Whatever he may have intended to say, there can be no mistake as to the meaning of the following sentence from Robert Pulleyn : " The species is the whole substance of individuals, and the whole species is the same in each individual : therefore the species is one substance, but its individuals many persons, and these many persons are that one substance."[1] The dialectician represented as saying this, ought to have been a prey to profound melancholy ; his samenesses are clearly in deplorable confusion. He makes his universal an individual, and then imposes upon it duties which

---

[1] *Species est tota substantia indiciduorum, totaque species eademque in singulis reperitur indi:iduis: itaque species una est substantia, ejus vero indi:idua multæ personæ, et hæ multæ personæ sunt illa una substantia. (Sentent.,* p. I. c. III.)—Quoted by Hauréau, I, p. 328.

no individual can fulfil with credit. It is to be one and yet not
one : distinct from something else, and yet identical with it.
It is to be a universal and not a universal. It is by no means
to be envied. The conceptualistic position of Abelard, that we
may gain a subjective universal by abstraction, but that only
individuals exist in reality, is open to the objections that I
advanced in discussing Nominalism. The position is supported[1]
by the argument that we may abstract the form from the sub-
stantial subject to which it is united, and consider it separately,
while in nature there is no such abstraction, the form and the
subject forming a united whole. To this one may answer, as I
have indicated above, that, whatever it may be united with, the
form in the several individuals is in some sense the same, or the
individuals would not be alike, and the concept would be of no
service in representing it. What is meant by such sameness? Is
it anything but sameness in sense fourth? When several objects
are the same in sense fourth, is not the element common to
them a universal? Why make this conceptualistic discrimination between things in mind and "real" things?

Finally, in passing from scholasticism, I would suggest that it
is conducive to clearness in thinking to bear in mind that when
Albert, or Thomas, or Duns, declares in favor of all three kinds
of universal, *ante rem*, *in re*, and *post rem*, he is declaring for
three things and not one. He is not at all in the position of the
old Platonic Realist ; but is rather, if I may so express it, a kind
of triple Aristotelian. One may perfectly well hold to all three
universals, by putting one in the mind of God, one in things, and
one in a human mind; but an individual may be given this three-
fold existence quite as well as a universal. In the old Realism
the problem of the universal called into existence a new sphere
of being. Here a new sphere of being, assumed upon extra-

---

[1] Hauréau, I, 380-381. The argument is taken from the *De Intellectibus*.

neous grounds, furnishes one more universal. The universals in the mind of God are not assumed as the object of the general name applied to twenty "real" objects. The object of this name is the *in re*. The *ante rem* universal cannot, then, be gotten as Plato got it. In this distinction between the different spheres of being we have an advance in reflection; but as I have said, on this new ground the individual may demand its rights. The *ante rem* Realism of the great scholastics of the thirteenth century should not be confounded with that of an earlier period. It is not open to the same objections. But on the other hand, it has not the same excuse for existence. It is a historical relic.

Sec. 29. The first of the moderns to whom I shall refer is Descartes. There are certain passages in the Meditations which will well illustrate the efforts made by this remarkable man in the direction of accurate analysis, as also the errors into which he fell through a confusion of the kinds of sameness. I shall quote from the second and third Meditations:

"Let us now accordingly consider the things which are commonly thought the easiest of all to know, and which are thought also to be the most distinctly known, that is, the bodies that we touch and see; not indeed bodies in general, for these general notions are usually a little more confused: but let us consider a single one of them. Let us take, for example, this bit of wax; it has just been taken from the hive; it has not yet lost the sweetness of the honey it contained; it still keeps something of the odor of the flowers from which it has been gathered; its color, its figure, its size, are apparent; it is hard, it is cold, it is easily handled, and if struck it gives a sound. In a word, everything that can make a body distinctly known is found in this one. But notice, while I speak, it is placed near the fire; what remained of savor and odor disappears, its color changes, its figure is lost, its size increases, it becomes liquid, grows hot, one can scarcely handle it, and when struck it no longer gives a sound. Does the same wax remain after this change? One must admit that it does; no one doubts it; no one judges otherwise. What then was it that was known with so much distinctness in this bit of wax? Certainly nothing that I perceived by means of the senses, for all the things which fall under taste, smell, sight, touch and hearing, are changed, and yet the same wax remains. Perhaps it was what I think now, namely, that this wax was neither the sweetness of honey, the agreeable odor of flowers, the whiteness, the figure, nor the sound, but only a body which a little before appeared to my senses under these forms, and which now appears to them under others. But to speak precisely, what do I imagine when I think it in this way? Let us consider it attentively, and abstracting all that does not belong to the wax, let us see what remains. Surely nothing remains but something extended, flexible and mutable. But what is that, flexible and mutable? Is it not that I imagine that this bit of wax, being round, is capable of becoming square and of changing from square to triangular? No, it is certainly not that, for I think it capable of an infinite number of similar changes; but I could not run through this infinite number by my imagination, and consequently this conception that I have of the wax is not due to the faculty of imagination. But what now is this extension? Is it not also unknown? For it becomes greater when the wax melts, greater when it boils, and still greater when the heat increases, and I could not conceive clearly and truly what wax is, if I did not think that even this bit that we are considering is capable of receiving more varieties of extension than I have ever imagined. It must then be admitted that I could not comprehend by imagination even what this bit of wax is, and that only my understanding can comprehend it. I say this particular bit of wax; for as for wax in general, it is still more evident. But what is this bit of wax that cannot be comprehended save by the understanding or the mind? It is certainly the same that I see, that I touch, that I imagine; it is, in a word, the same that I have always thought it from the beginning. But, what is important to note here is, that my perception is not a sensation of sight, nor of touch, nor an act of the imagination, and it has never been this, although it may have seemed so before; but it is merely an intuition (*inspection*) of the mind, which may be imperfect and confused as it was before, or clear and distinct as it is at present, according as my attention is directed more or less to the elements in it, and of which it is composed.

"However, I cannot be too much surprised when I consider the weakness of my mind and its proneness to be carried insensibly into error. For even when I consider all this in my own mind, and without using language, the words arrest me, and I am almost deceived by the terms in common use; for we say that we see the same wax if it be present, and not that we judge that it is the same, from its having the same color and figure; whence I might be tempted to conclude that one knows the wax by the sight of the eyes, and not merely by the intuition of the mind, were it not that, in looking from a window at men passing in the street, I say that I see men, just as I say that I see the wax; and yet what do I see from this window except hats and cloaks which might cover machines moved by springs? But I judge that they are men, and thus comprehend only by the power of judging, which is in my mind, what I thought I saw with my eyes."[1]

[1] Méditation Deuxième.—Ed. Simon, Paris, 1860, pp. 76-78.

In this extract the author attempts to distinguish between what is thought and what is perceived by the senses or imagined. Had he remained within the sphere of the immediately known, one could not have objected to such a distinction. Sameness in sense third is something highly complex, implying that elaboration of mental elements which we call thought. It is quite just to distinguish the notion "a bit of wax" from any single sense experience or picture of the imagination. In doing this Descartes was searching for sameness in sense third. But when he leaves the sphere of consciousness, and assumes that what remains the same in the bit of wax is something distinct from the sum total of experiences, as men are distinct from their garments, he falls into error. It is against this that the criticism in the text is directed.

What Descartes is feeling for in this is sameness in sense third. When we use the words "a bit of wax," we do not have in mind a single experience. The wax in a solid and the wax in a liquid state is to us the same wax. I have pointed out what the word same, so used, means. It means that these two experiences are recognized as belonging to the one group or series of experiences ; and the wax, completely known, is the sum total of the series. Descartes saw very well that the two experiences under discussion are not strictly identical (the same in sense first), and he saw also that they are very unlike. He naturally asked, In what then are they the same ? or, what is there that is here the same? And, instead of accepting the fact that such a sameness as this cannot be reduced to one of the others, he solved the problem by passing from the experiences, the "hats and cloaks," to a "real" thing underlying. In other words, to explain the sameness of two experiences of a bit of wax, sameness in sense third, he assumed "real" wax, which is the same with the experiences which represent it only in sense seventh. This real wax, or something in it, he supposes to remain the same on two occasions. It is this to which he makes the mind refer when it calls the wax the same. But when a man advances statements about a bit of wax, his information rests ultimately upon his expeences, if it be grounded at all. From the experience one infers the "real" thing, and not *vice versa*. No one knew this better than Descartes, with his fundamental principle of the certainty of consciousness and the uncertainty of what is "external." He got his "real" world by a process of reasoning, and put it in a realm wholly cut off from direct observation. This being the case, one cannot but wonder at his inconsistency in the present instance. Is one to remain in doubt whether a piece of wax felt to be hard, and then melted before the fire, is the same, until one has had some means of discovering that the same "real" wax is present on the two occasions? How is one to find out whether "real" wax is ever present unless he infer its presence from some experience? And how is one to know that the same "real" wax is present on two occasions unless he infer it from the fact that what is directly perceived on the two occasions is the same in some sense of the word? Whatever sameness there is rests ultimately for its evidence upon the experiences. There is nothing else to judge from. The reasoning, which would base the sameness of what is experienced upon the sameness of a corresponding "real" thing, when the sameness of this latter is to be inferred from the former, reminds one of the stupid argument, still occasionally met with, which would infer a God from data of consciousness, and then found a belief in the veracity of consciousness upon the goodness of God. One may believe, if one please, that, when we have two distinct experiences so connected that we call them two perceptions of the same wax, there is in some way connected with them a bit of "real" wax which remains in some sense the same. But one should never suppose that any given experienced wax is proved the same by reference to this. It is judged the same upon observation.

Descartes then was inconsistent with his own principles when he made this jump to a new sphere of being. The sameness of the experienced object is ultimate ; the only pertinent question is, what does it mean? It means, as I have said, that the wax hard and the wax soft are the same in sense third. But sameness in sense third admits of wide dissimilarities in the experiences it unites into the notion of the one object. Descartes looked for a sameness without these dissimilarities. He would reduce sense third to sense first, or, perhaps, to sense second· To do this he must go behind the experiences to a "real" thing, which is to remain the same as a proxy for what is evidently variable. This makeshift is only satisfactory to one who overlooks, or allows to fall into the background, the plain fact that representative and thing represented are two separate things and not to be confused; that is, who confuses sameness in sense first with sameness in sense seventh. Descartes distinguished carefully between ideas and external things, but he sometimes overlooked the distinction. "But what is this bit of wax that cannot be comprehended save by the understanding or the mind? It is certainly the same that I see, that I touch, that I imagine; it is, in a word, the same that I have always thought it from the beginning." How ambiguous! is it the same in sense first or sense seventh? The sentence following would indicate sense seventh, but the spirit of the whole discussion would argue for sense first. One must delude oneself into believing that one can get at "real" wax directly, in some way or other, or one cannot think of making it an ultimate ground of reasoning. Descartes, like so many others, would seem to have vibrated between a clear consciousness that ideas and "real" things are distinct, belonging to different worlds, and a confused belief that they belong to the one world, and that "real" things are open to direct observation.

I shall take still another extract from this author. It contains similar errors.

"Now, among these ideas, some appear to me to be inborn, others to be foreign and to come from without, and still others to be made and invented by myself. For, as to the faculty of conceiving that which, in general, one calls a thing, or a truth, or a thought, it appears to me that I do not get that from any other source than my own nature; but if now I hear a sound, if I see the sun, if I feel the heat, up to the present I have judged that these sensations proceed from things which exist without me; and lastly, it seems to me that syrens, hippogriffs, and all similar chimeras are fictions and inventions of my mind. But perhaps I can persuade myself, that all these ideas belong to the class of those that I call foreign, and that come to me from without, or that they are all innate, or else that they are all created by myself; for I have not yet clearly discovered their true source. And my chief duty here is to consider, touching those which seem to come from objects without me, what reasons I have for thinking them like their objects.

"The first of the reasons is that I seem to be taught to do so by nature; and the second, that I perceive that these ideas are not dependent upon my will; for often they present themselves to me in spite of me, as now, whether I wish it or not, I feel heat, and consequently am persuaded that this sensation or idea of heat is produced in me by something different from me, to wit : by the heat of the fire by which I am sitting. And I cannot see that anything is more reasonable than to judge that this external object emits and impresses upon me its resemblance rather than anything else.

" Now I must see if these reasons are sufficiently strong and convincing. When I say that I seem to be taught so by nature, I mean merely by this word nature a certain inclination which leads me to believe it, and not a natural light which gives me certain knowledge that it is true. But these two ways of speaking are very different, for I cannot doubt anything that the natural light shows me to be true, as it has just shown me that from the fact of my doubting I may infer my existence; inasmuch as I have not in me any other faculty or power of distinguishing the true from the false to teach me that what this light shows me to be true is not true, and in which I may have as much confidence as in it. But as concerns inclinations which also seem to me natural, I have often remarked, when it has been a question of choice between virtues and vices, that they do not less incline to evil than to good ; it follows that I have no more reason to follow them when the true and the false are in question. And as for the other reason, which is that these ideas must come from without, since they are not dependent on my will, I do not find it more convincing. For while these inclinations of which I have just spoken are in me, notwithstanding that they are not always in harmony with my will, perhaps there is in me some faculty or power capable of producing these ideas without the aid of external things, although it is yet unknown to me; as indeed it has always seemed to me up to this time that when I sleep they are thus formed in me without the aid of the objects they represent. Finally, even should I admit that they are caused by these objects, it does not necessarily follow that they must be like them. On the contrary, I have often remarked in many instances, that there is a great difference between an object and its idea: as, for example, I find in me two very different ideas of the sun; the one has its source in the senses, and should be placed in the class of those which I have said above come from without, and from this it seems to me very small; the other has it origin in astronomical reasonings, that is to say, in certain notions which are inborn, or else formed in some way or other by myself, and from this it seems to me many times greater than the whole earth. Surely, these two ideas which I have of the sun cannot both be like the same sun; and reason convinces me that the one which is derived directly from its appearance is the one which is most unlike it. All of which proves to me that, up to this hour, it has not been by a sure and premeditated judgment, but merely by a blind and rash impulse, that I have been led to believe that there are things without me, and different from my being, which, by the organs of my senses, or by whatever other means, convey to me their ideas or images, and impress upon me their resemblances."[1]

From the earlier portions of this extract one may see how clearly Descartes distinguished between the idea, or the thing immediately known, and the external thing which he assumed as corresponding to the idea; from the latter part one may see how he sometimes confounded them. He finds that he may doubt whether ideas have any external correlatives; and, granting that they have, whether the two resemble each other at all. All this would imply that "external" things are completely cut off from observation. And yet he states with *naïveté* that he has "often remarked in many instances that there is a great ·difference between an object and its idea." Now, if this can really be remarked in many instances, the doubt as to the existence of objects would seem to be groundless. How can it be remarked? On this point Descartes is silent. He has evidently fallen back upon the popular notion that under favorable circumstances one can get a look at a "real" thing, just as it is. The "reason" which convinces him that the astronomer's notion of the sun is the true notion is nothing but this. It could certainly not be deduced from his only argument for the existence of external things—the veracity of God. How does he know, that in giving us several different ideas of the sun, God has chosen to have this one only resemble it? It is a pure assumption. Reason is of service when one has something to go upon; but in the absence of premises it will not carry one far. This assumption is an illustration of what I had occasion to remark upon in criticizing Pyrrho; of the fact that, from the series of possible perceptions which we group together as one object, we are apt to select one, to us for some reason the most satisfactory one, and to regard it as more truly representing the object than the others. Descartes has followed this impulse, and made this perception the best representative of the "real" object. Had he always distinguished sameness in sense first from sameness in sense seventh, he would have seen how purely gratuitous is his assumption.

The statement, too, that two different ideas of the sun cannot both resemble the same sun, shows how little he comprehended what it meant by the word same when used in the third sense. If by the sun we mean a whole series of possible perceptions, perhaps quite unlike each other, but all united and related in certain ways, there is nothing to prevent very dissimilar things from being like the same sun. Each of them need only resemble a single link in the series. By the words "the same sun" Descartes meant the same in sense first, but this sins against the proper meaning of the term. The difficulty is self-created.

Descartes' sun reminds me of Berkeley's moon. This latter writer clearly perceived that there may be multiplicity and diversity where one attributes sameness in sense third. Note the following :

"But for a fuller explication of this point, and to show that the immediate objects of sight are not so much as the ideas or resemblances of things placed at a distance, it is requisite that we look nearer into the matter, and carefully observe what is meant in common discourse when one says that which he sees is at a distance from him. Suppose, for example, that looking at the moon I should say it were fifty or sixty semidiameters of the earth distant from me. Let us see what moon this is spoken of. It is plain it cannot be the visible moon, or anything like the visible moon, or that I see—which is only a round, luminous plain, of about thirty visible points in diameter. For, in case I am carried from the place where I stand directly toward the moon, it is manifest the object varies still as I go on ; and, by the time that I am advanced fifty or sixty semidiameters of the earth, I shall be so far from being near a small, round, luminous flat that I shall perceive nothing like it—this object having long since disappeared, and, if I would recover it, it must be by going back to the earth from whence I set out."[1]

So much for dissimilar experiences of the same object. And Berkeley is not impelled to assume an external something to explain how the object can be the same under the circumstances. The case, he finds, stands thus:

"Having of a long time experienced certain ideas perceivable by touch—as distance, tangible figure, and solidity—to have been connected with certain ideas of sight, I do, upon perceiving these ideas of sight, forthwith conclude what tangible ideas are, by the wonted ordinary course of nature, like to follow. Looking at an object, I perceive a certain visible figure and color, with some degree of faintness and other circumstances, which, from what I have formerly observed, determine me to think that if I advance forward so many paces, miles, etc., I shall be affected with such and such ideas of touch."[2]

And need one ask a clearer illustration of sameness in sense third than the case of the coach, which occurs in the following section:

"Sitting in my study I hear a coach drive along the street; I look through the casement and see it; I walk out and enter into it. Thus, common speech would incline one to think I heard, saw, and touched the same thing, to wit, the coach. It is, nevertheless, certain the ideas intromitted by each sense are widely different and distinct from each other; but, having been observed constantly to go together, they are spoken of as one and the same thing."

SEC. 30. It would be easy to select from Spinoza, that master of reasonings apparently very exact but really very loose, many good instances of confused samenesses. I shall confine myself

---

[1] "Essay towards a New Theory of Vision." Sec. 44. Works: ed. Fraser. Oxford 1871. Vol. I, p. 53.

[2] *Ibid.*, § 45.

to a single one, his argument to prove that every substance is necessarily infinite. It is the eighth proposition in Part I of the Ethics.

"There cannot be more than one substance with the same attribute, and this exists of its own nature. It belongs, then, to its nature to exist either as finite or as infinite. But it cannot be finite, for then it would have to be limited by another of the same kind, which would also necessarily exist; there would then be two substances with the same attribute, which is absurd. It is, therefore, infinite."[1]

Among its defects this argument includes a confusion of sameness in sense fourth with sameness in sense first. Attribute Spinoza has defined as that which is conceived as the essence of substance. Mode is a modification of substance. Two substances, he has argued, cannot be distinguished from each other by their modifications, for substance is prior to its modifications, and we may set these aside and consider it as it is in itself. Substances cannot then, be distinguished except by their attributes ; and if the attribute be the same, how can we say that there are two substances? There cannot, consequently, be two substances with the same attribute.

But, the argument continues, since there cannot be two substances with the same attribute, every substance must be infinite ; for, to be finite, a thing must be limited by something : and nothing can be limited except by a thing of the same kind (for example, a material thing cannot be limited by a thought). But if a thing be limited by another thing of the same kind, the thing limited and the thing limiting have the same attribute. It fol-

---

[1] *Substantia unius attributi non nisi unica existit, et ad ipsius naturam pertinet existere. Erit ergo de ipsius natura vel finita vel infinita existere. At non finita. Nam deberet terminari ab alia eiusdem natura, quæ etiam necessario deberet existere ; adeoque darentur duæ substantia eiusdem attributi, quod est absurdum. Existit ergo infinita :* q. e. d.— *Ethices, Pars prima ; VIII. Omnis substantia est necessario infinita.* Leipzig, 1875, p. 84.

lows that they are not two things, but one. The thing in question is not limited but infinite.

In criticizing this, I may call attention, in passing, to the highly disputable and gratuitously assumed premise, that, to be finite, a thing must be limited by something. If this be denied, the ground of the reasoning is removed; while, if it be granted, no argument is needed to prove that *something* is infinite, for one has only said in other words that all limits must be limits within something. The question is begged at once. With this, however, I am not concerned. What interests me is this: The argument assumes a limited thing and a something beyond it, and then asserts that they are one. But two things of the same kind in different places, or marked as different by distinctions of any sort, are readily distinguished as two. To come to the concrete, extension conceived as on this side of a point and extension conceived as beyond the point are not extension simply, but "this" extension and "that" extension. They are the same only in sense fourth, not in sense first. We have here not merely the attribute extension, but the further elements "this" and "that." The conclusion, then, that what we started out with is infinite, is wholly unwarranted. It is not this that is infinite, but this with something else which is to some degree like it, although not wholly so. That is to say, the thing assumed as finite can only be proved to be infinite by confounding two samenesses. The thing proved to be infinite is a new object including it and what it is assumed to presuppose. If it be not permissible to make this distinction between the object assumed as finite, for the sake of the argument, and the object which is proved to be infinite, it is also not permissible to assert that an object to be finite "would have to be limited by another of the same kind." If the two are one, these words are meaningless. If they are not one, one cannot conclude from the argument that every substance is necessarily infinite, but only that something is necessarily infinite, a conclusion already given in the single premise that what is limited must be limited by something of the same kind. As a matter of fact, Spinoza retains in his argument not only the attribute, but the mode, the "this" and the "beyond this;" and then he overlooks the mode and considers merely the attribute, which gives him strict identity. This procedure we have met before in the dispute concerning universals.

Sec. 31. In the former part of my monograph I have mentioned Locke's confusion of sameness in sense seventh with sameness in sense first. I shall now quote a few sections from the "Essay concerning Human Understanding" to show how significant his error is, and to what an extent it is responsible for his position regarding ideas, things, and substance. My extracts are from the eleventh chapter of the fourth book, entitled "Of our Knowledge of the Existence of Other Things." Locke argues as follows :[1]

"The knowledge of our own being we have by intuition. The existence of a God reason clearly makes known to us, as has been shown.

" The knowledge of the existence of any other thing we can have only by sensation : for there being no necessary connection of real existence with any idea a man hath in his memory, nor of any other existence but that of God, with the existence of any particular man ; no particular man can know the existence of any other being, but only when by actual operating upon him it makes itself perceived by him. For the having the idea of anything in our mind no more proves the existence of that thing, than the picture of a man evidences his being in the world, or the visions of a dream make thereby a true history.

" It is therefore the actual receiving of ideas from without, that gives us notice of the existence of other things, and makes

---

[1] Locke's Essays, Philadelphia, 1846, p. 415, *et seq.*

us know that something doth exist at that time without us, which causes that idea in us, though perhaps we neither know nor consider how it does it : for it takes not from the certainty of our senses, and the ideas we receive by them, that we know not the manner wherein they are produced, *v. g.*, whilst I write this I have, by the paper affecting my eyes, that idea produced in my mind which, whatever object causes, I call white ; by which I know that that quality or accident (*i. e.*, whose appearance before my eyes always causes that idea) doth really exist, and hath a being without me. And of this, the greatest assurance I can possibly have, and to which my faculties can attain, is the testimony of my eyes, which are the proper and sole judges of this thing, whose testimony I have reason to rely on as so certain, that I can no more doubt, whilst I write this, that I see white and black, and that something really exists that causes that sensation in me, than that I write or move my hand : which is a certainty as great as human nature is capable of, concerning the existence of anything but a man's self alone, and of God.

"The notice we have by our senses of the existing of things without us, though it be not altogether so certain as our intuitive knowledge, or the deductions of our reason, employed about the clear abstract ideas of our own minds ; yet it is an assurance that deserves the name of knowledge. If we persuade ourselves that our faculties act and inform us right, concerning the existence of those objects that affect them, it cannot pass for an ill-grounded confidence : for I think nobody can, in earnest, be so sceptical as to be uncertain of the existence of those things which he sees and feels. At least, he that can doubt so far (whatever he may have with his own thoughts) will never have any controversy with me ; since he can never be sure I say anything contrary to his own opinion. As to myself, I think God has given me assurance enough of the existence of things with-

out me ; since by their different application I can produce in
myself both pleasure and pain, which is one great concernment
of my present state. This is certain, the confidence that our
faculties do not herein deceive us is the greatest assurance we
are capable of, concerning the existence of material beings. For
we cannot act anything but by our faculties ; nor talk of knowledge itself, but by the helps of those faculties which are fitted
to apprehend even what knowledge is. But besides the assurance we have from our senses themselves, that they do not err
in the information they give us, of the existence of things without us, when they are affected by them, we are farther confirmed
in this assurance by other concurrent reasons.

"First, it is plain those perceptions are produced in us by
exterior causes affecting our senses : because those that want the
organs of any sense never can have the ideas belonging to that
sense produced in their minds. This is too evident to be doubted :
and therefore we cannot but be assured that they come in by
the organs of that sense, and no other way. The organs themselves, it is plain, do not produce them ; for then the eyes of a
man in the dark would produce colors, and his nose smell roses
in the winter : but we see nobody gets the relish of a pine apple
till he goes to the Indies, where it is, and tastes it.

"Secondly, because sometimes I find that I cannot avoid the
having those ideas produced in my mind. For though when my
eyes are shut, or windows fast, I can at pleasure recall to my
mind the ideas of light, or the sun, which former sensations had
lodged in my memory ; so I can at pleasure lay by that idea, and
take into my view that of the smell of a rose, or taste of sugar.
But if I turn my eyes at noon towards the sun, I cannot avoid
the ideas which the light, or sun, then produces in me. So that
there is a manifest difference between the ideas laid up in my
memory (over which, if they were there only, I should have

constantly the same power to dispose of them, and lay them by at pleasure), and those which force themselves upon me, and I cannot avoid having. And therefore it must needs be some exterior cause, and the brisk acting of some objects without me, whose efficacy I cannot resist, that produces those ideas in my mind, whether I will or no. Besides, there is nobody who doth not perceive the difference in himself between contemplating the sun, as he hath the idea of it in his memory, and actually looking upon it; of which two his perception is so distinct, that few of his ideas are more distinguishable one from another. And therefore, he hath certain knowledge, that they are not both memory, or the actions of his mind, and fancies only within him; but that actual seeing hath a cause without.

"Thirdly, add to this, that many of those ideas are produced in us with pain, which afterward we remember without the least offense. Thus the pain of heat or cold, when the idea of it is revived in our minds, gives us no disturbance; which, when felt, was very troublesome, and is again when actually repeated; which is occasioned by the disorder the external object causes in our bodies when applied to it. And we remember the pains of hunger, thirst, or the headache, without any pain at all; which would either never disturb us, or else constantly do it, as often as we thought of it, were there nothing more but ideas floating in our minds, and appearances entertaining our fancies, without the real existence of things affecting us from abroad. The same may be said of pleasure accompanying several actual sensations, and though mathematical demonstrations depend not upon sense, yet the examining them by diagrams gives great credit to the evidence of our sight, and seems to give it a certainty approaching to that of demonstration itself. For it would be very strange that a man should allow it for an undeniable truth, that two angles of a figure, which he measures by lines and angles of a diagram, should be bigger one than the other; and yet doubt of the existence of those lines and angles, which by looking on he makes use of to measure that by.

"Fourthly, our senses in many cases bear witness to the truth of each other's report, concerning the existence of sensible things without us. He that sees a fire may, if he doubt whether it be anything more than a bare fancy, feel it too; and be convinced by putting his hand in it: which certainly could never be put into such exquisite pain by a bare idea or phantom, unless that the pain be a fancy too, which yet he cannot, when the burn is well, by raising the idea of it, bring upon himself again.

"Thus I see, whilst I write this, I can change the appearance of the paper: and by designing the letters tell beforehand what new idea it shall exhibit the very next moment, by barely drawing my pen over it: which will neither appear (let me fancy as much as I will), if my hands stand still; or though I move my pen, if my eyes be shut: nor, when those characters are once made on the paper, can I choose afterward but see them as they are: that is, have the ideas of such letters as I have made. Whence it is manifest, that they are not barely the sport and play of my own imagination, when I find that the characters that were made at the pleasure of my own thought, do not obey them; nor yet cease to be, whenever I shall fancy it; but continue to affect the senses constantly and regularly, according to the figures I made them. To which if we will add, that the sight of those shall, from another man, draw such sounds as I beforehand design they shall stand for; there will be little reason left to doubt that those words I write do really exist without me, when they cause a long series of regular sounds to affect my ears, which could not be the effect of my imagination, nor could my memory retain them in that order."

This is quite a long citation, but I have given it at length because it may stand as the type of by far the greater part of the objections urged against Idealism, and because a better instance of the confusion of two samenesses could scarcely be desired. Notice how constantly it is assumed that the thing given in perception is the "real" thing, a thing which is, nevertheless, characterized as distinct from, and the cause of, the idea.

At the outset Locke distinguishes well enough between the idea and the "external" thing. The having the idea of any thing in the mind, he declares, no more proves the existence of that thing than the picture of a man evidences his being in the world. It is only the receiving of ideas from without that gives us notice of things as causes of the ideas. It would seem quite fair here to ask how we know that some ideas come from without? Of course, if the realm of the "without" were open to inspection, the question could be answered at once. But it is not open to inspection—certainly not to a consistent Lockian. How, then, may I distinguish ideas coming from without from other ideas? No ideas are perceived until they are what Locke would call "within."

The appeal to the testimony of the eyes needs examination. To what eyes does one appeal? The immediately known or idea-eyes, or the "external" organs whose existence is the matter of dispute? Surely not to the last, for it is only as a result of the argument that we may assume these at all. And what hand is it so certain that I move in writing? The complex of ideas immediately known, or the something beyond, whose existence is to be established? If it be the latter, all discussion is unnecessary. If, on the other hand, the eyes and the hand concerned are ideas, it is not clear how the appeal to them can be of any service. Does a sense give anything but sensations? And if the very sense organ as immediately known be a group of sensations, how can the testimony of a sense land one in a world beyond that of sensations? And the argument that God has given me assurance of the existence of things without me, since by applying them to myself I can produce in myself pain and pleasure, presupposes that I can apply such things to myself and know that I am doing so. If this be the fact, it is trifling to discuss whether things I move to and fro exist. If, however, it is still to be proved that there are such things, and that they are moved to and fro, the argument is wholly baseless. Locke here makes appeal to the common experience that certain objects applied to the body cause pleasure, and certain others pain ; a fact which no reasonable man would think of denying or questioning, as it is matter of daily observation. But in such experiences, all that is immediately evident is that an object immediately perceived (Locke's idea) is applied to another object immediately perceived (idea) with a resulting (idea) pain. Whether or not certain duplicates of the things immediately known are brought into a peculiar conjunction at the same time is wholly problematic, and would seem to remain so until some evidence be advanced of the existence of such duplicates. This argument on the part of our author shows most clearly that for the time being he lost the distinction between ideas and "real " things. They are the same in sense seventh ; he assumed them to be the same in sense first. He falls into this error again and again.

The general appeal to the testimony of the senses is followed by four special arguments. According to the first of these, it is plain that perceptions are produced in us by exterior causes affecting our senses, "because those that want the organs of any sense never can have the ideas belonging to that sense produced in their minds." This is supposed to prove that they come in by the organs of that sense, and in no other way. But here again one may ask, What is meant by the organs of any sense? If the "real" external organ be meant, one may object

that its existence has not yet been proved. If the organ immediately known be meant, one has only called attention to the fact
that certain ideas are a *sine qua non* to the existence of certain
other ideas. How this tends to prove the existence of something distinct from ideas is not apparent. Locke's impulse in
this argument finds its source in our common experience that
bodily organs immediately perceived are proved by observation
to be prerequisites to the experiencing of ideas. We see a
given object in a certain relation to a normal human body, and
we infer an idea of the object connected with that body. We
say the man has an idea of the object, and can only infer the
object itself. We connect the idea with some particular part of
his body, and regard this as the medium through which he gains
the idea. All this is reasonable enough. It is well to remember, however, that in all this the "real" object is not observed
to play any part. The object which I certainly see in relation
to the body which I certainly see is what Locke would call an
idea. The man's body is an idea. The idea which I assume the
man to have is to me, if I remain within the sphere of the observable, an idea of the (idea) object I see. If I am to get any
"real" object at all it is not by reference to observation or experience. If I am to get it by inference, some ground must be
furnished for inference. Again Locke has confounded the
observable with the "real." It is only on this ground that the
appeal to the sense organ has any force.

The second and the third arguments busy themselves to show
that there are unmistakable differences between ideas which
have their origin in the "brisk acting" of objects without and
ideas of memory or imagination. The two classes are shown
to be distinct, and it is very properly held that ideas of different
kinds should not be confounded. But the statement, that ideas
may be divided into two classes, is a very different one from the

statement that the two classes differ in that one has external correlates and the other has not. One may admit all the distinctions which Locke makes in the field of ideas; and, it being once proved that such distinctions imply a world of "real" things in relation to certain ideas, may grant very readily that these ideas have corresponding to them "real" things, or that ideas caused by "real" things differ by such and such marks from other ideas. But, until it be proved that the marks in question do give a right to infer "real" things, it should not be assumed that any given class of ideas is caused by "real" things. What is to be discovered is assumed. And it is assumed here, as above, because Locke could not keep distinct the two classes of things. He is capable of saying, "But if I turn my eyes at noon towards the sun, I cannot avoid the ideas which the light, or sun, then produces in me," when the whole dispute is over the question whether there be a "real" sun toward which "real" eyes may be turned. How does he know that he is turning his eyes toward the sun? Does he not see it up there? Is he not "actually looking upon it?" His error is too plain to overlook. But if one could doubt his confusion of the two suns, the apparent and the "real," his illustration from the diagrams used in mathematical demonstration would lay the doubt once for all. "Real" lines exist, "for it would be very strange that a man should allow it for an undeniable truth, that two angles of a figure, which he measures by lines and angles of a diagram, should be bigger one than the other; and yet doubt of the existence of those lines and angles, which by looking on he makes use of to measure that by." The English is not as bad as the reasoning.

The fourth argument is derived from the fact that one sense supports the testimony of another. "He that sees a fire may, if he doubt whether it be anything more than a bare fancy, feel it too." A bare fancy, Locke is sure, would not cause such acute pain. This comes back to the second and third arguments and may be criticized in the same way. If one could refer to a single observation of the fact that "real" things do not accompany ideas of the fancy and that they do accompany ideas of a different class, the argument would be unobjectionable. Wanting this observation, or something to take its place, nothing is proved. And as to the senses helping each other to "real" things, if each sense only gives the idea appropriate to it, it is not easy to see how two together prove more than one alone. In this section, too, Locke is assuming that "real" things belong to the world of things immediately perceived. He can, he says, make what characters he pleases on the paper before him, but once having made them, cannot choose but see them as they are. "Whence it is manifest, that they are not barely the sport and play of my own imagination, when I find that the characters that were made at the pleasure of my own thought, do not obey them; nor yet cease to be, whenever I shall fancy it; but continue to affect the senses constantly and regularly, according to the figures I made them." That is, the ideas which he concludes not to be ideas of imagination are the things "which continue to affect the senses," or the "real" things. There is little wonder that this author believed in "real" things.

SEC. 32. Excellent work has been done by Berkeley in distinguishing samenesses. His treatment of sameness in sense third I have already quoted. His discussion of the infinite divisibility of finite lines,[1] a matter of which I shall speak more fully later, again brings out sense third. Almost his whole philosophy consists in the endeavor to keep clearly in mind the significance of sense seventh, and to develop what it implies. On the other hand, he has fallen into the error of confusing

[1] " A Treatise Concerning the Principles of Human Knowledge," §§ 123-132. Ed. Fraser, Vol. I, pp. 220-225.

sense first and sense sixth, and of using this confusion to silence an objection to his doctrine.

He takes up in the "Principles," for the purpose of refuting it, the objection that his doctrine makes things every moment annihilated and created anew.[1] This, he argues, "will not be found reasonably charged on the principles we have premised, so as in truth to make any objection at all against our notions. For, though we hold indeed the objects of sense to be nothing else but ideas which cannot exist unperceived; yet we may not hence conclude they have no existence except only while they are perceived by us, since there may be some other spirit that perceives them though we do not. Wherever bodies are said to have no existence without the mind, I would not be understood to mean this or that particular mind, but all minds whatsoever. It does not therefore follow from the foregoing principles that bodies are annihilated and created every moment, or exist not at all during the intervals between our perception of them."

To the reader of Mill it is clear enough that Berkeley is not content to assume potential existence as an integral part of the life history of an object. It seems odd that he should not do so, as he has himself pointed out the double sense of the word exist.[2] However, he demands actual existence. Any lapse in the actual existence of the immediate object seems to him a destruction of the object. He has the common feeling that it is contrary to nature that things should be destroyed and created from moment to moment. They must exist continuously. They evidently do not actually exist continuously in the one mind. So he assumes that, during the periods of their absence from one mind, they must exist in another: otherwise they could not be said to exist at all.

[1] §§ 45-48, pp. 178-180.   [2] "Principles," § 3, p. 157.

Of course, all this assumes that the objects in one mind are identically (sense first) the objects in another. If they be recognized as two distinct things, belonging to different worlds — worlds so different that what is in one can enter the other only through its representative—the whole argument is seen to be fallacious. One can no more make a consistent whole of elements taken from two different consciousnesses, than one can piece out a grief with a smell. The attempt is the result of overlooking the duality implied in sameness in sense sixth.

SEC. 33. There is a clear and forcible passage in John Stuart Mill's "System of Logic," in which he distinguishes certain samenesses from certain others. It is to be regretted that he dismissed the subject with so slight an examination, for it could not but have gained by a careful analysis at the hands of this keen man. I quote more particularly to bring out what Mill has to say about sameness in sense second.

" While speaking of resemblance, it is necessary to take notice of an ambiguity of language, against which scarcely any one is sufficiently on his guard. Resemblance, when it exists in the highest degree of all, amounting to undistinguishableness, is often called identity, and the two similar things are said to be the same. I say often, not always ; for we do not say that two visible objects, two persons, for instance, are the same, because they are so much alike that one might be mistaken for the other: but we constantly use this mode of expression when speaking of feelings; as when I say that the sight of any object gives me the *same* sensation or emotion to-day that it did yesterday, or the *same* which it gives to some other person. This is evidently an incorrect application of the word *same;* for the feeling which I had yesterday is gone, never to return ; what I have to-day is another feeling, exactly like the former, perhaps, but distinct from it ; and it is evident that two different persons cannot be experiencing the same feeling, in the sense in which we say that they are both sitting at the same table. By a similar ambiguity we say, that two persons are ill of the *same* disease; that two persons hold the *same* office; not in the sense in which we say that they are engaged in the same adventure, or sailing in the same ship, but in the sense that they fill offices exactly similar, though, perhaps, in distant places. Great confusion of ideas is often produced, and many fallacies engendered, in otherwise enlightened understandings, by not being sufficiently alive to the fact (in itself not always to be avoided), that they use the same name to express ideas so different as those of identity and undistinguishable resemblance."[1]

It will be seen that Mill here draws a line between sameness in sense first and the samenesses in which there is an element of duality. He also draws attention to the fact—a fact to which I have already referred—that successive mental elements, considered in themselves, are more likely to be confounded than material things, though these last may be quite as closely similar. Language shows how men overlook the duality of two similar feelings which differ only in time. They may speak of two similar objects as the same, as they frequently do, and yet they will not usually lose the sense of their twoness. They say *these* objects are the same. But when they compare a feeling experienced to-day with one experienced yesterday, they say *this* is the same feeling I had yesterday. There is nothing in the language used to indicate duality at all.

I have said that, in the extract given, a line is drawn between samenesses which imply duality and the sameness which does not; and yet such illustrations are used to represent the latter as a man, a table, and a ship—objects which are the same in sense third as well as in sense first, and which consequently

[1] "A System of Logic," Book I, Chap. III, § 11, N. Y., 1882, p. 62.

imply duality, in some sense of the word. But, if one is not considering single members of the chain of experiences which, taken
together, we call a man, but is considering the whole group as a
unit, this difficulty disappears. This is evidently what Mill has
in mind, and he cannot be taxed with inconsistency. One may,
however, object to the statement that it is an improper use of
the word same to speak of things merely similar as the same.
The word has many meanings, and we can hardly say that any
one of them is illegitimate. It is merely illegitimate to confound
them. And one should not take quite literally the description of
resemblance in the highest degree as "amounting to undistinguishableness." Strict undistinguishableness removes all duality, and consequently makes impossible what we call resemblance
or similarity. To be similar, things must be distinguished as
two. Finally, one may object to a treatment of samenesses
which merely groups them into two classes, when there are at
least seven kinds that should, in the interests of clear thinking,
be kept separate. It is only by carefully marking such distinctions that fallacious reasonings are to be avoided. As, however,
this discussion of samenesses is merely a side issue where it occurs
in the Logic, it would perhaps be unjust to blame Mill for not
going into it more fully.

SEC. 34. At this point I leave the realms of the dead and
emerge into the land of the living. The errors that I have
been criticizing still live, and it would not be difficult to glean a
goodly number of them from the authors of our day. I shall be
moderate, and will content myself with one or two representative instances.

It would be surprising if as loose and incautious a reasoner as
Mr. Herbert Spencer did not furnish some examples of confused
samenesses. To certain of his errors in this direction I have
briefly referred in the earlier part of my monograph. Here I

shall treat of him a little more at length, though even here it is impossible to do justice to the subject, as that would involve my quoting and commenting upon at least a large part of the first division of the " First Principles." I shall take only the conclusion of the argument by which he establishes the existence of his " Unknowable," or "Inscrutable Power," or "Ulti. mate Cause," or "Unseen Reality," or "Absolute." This contains two confusions of no little significance. Mr. Spencer writes :

" Hence our firm belief in objective reality—a belief which metaphysical criticisms cannot for a moment shake. When we are taught that a piece of matter, regarded by us as existing externally, cannot be really known, but that we can know only certain impressions produced on us, we are yet, by the relativity of our thought, compelled to think of these in relation to a positive cause—the notion of a real existence which generated these impressions becomes nascent. If it be proved to us that every notion of a real existence which we can frame is utterly incon‾ sistent with itself—that matter, however conceived by us, cannot be matter as it actually is, our conception, though transfigured, is not destroyed : there remains the sense of reality, dissociated as far as possible from those special forms under which it was before represented in thought. Though Philosophy condemns successively each attempted conception of the Absolute—though it proves to us that the Absolute is not this, nor that, nor that—though in obedience to it we negative, one after another, each idea as it arises ; yet, as we cannot expel the entire contents of consciousness, there ever remains behind an element which passes into new shapes. The continual negation of each particular form and limit, simply results in the more or less complete abstraction of all forms and limits ; and so ends in an indefinite consciousness of the unformed and unlimited.

"And here we come face to face with the ultimate difficulty—
How can there possibly be constituted a consciousness of the
unformed and unlimited, when, by its very nature, consciousness is possible only under forms and limits? If every consciousness of existence is a consciousness of existence as conditioned, then how, after the negation of conditions, can there be
any residuum? Though not directly withdrawn by the with-
drawal of its conditions, must not the raw material of consciousness be withdrawn by implication? Must it not vanish when
the conditions of its existence vanish? That there must be a
solution of this difficulty is manifest; since even those who
would put it, do, as already shown, admit that we have some such
consciousness; and the solution appears to be that above
shadowed forth. Such consciousness is not, and cannot be,
constituted by any single mental act; but is the product of
many mental acts. In each concept there is an element
which persists. It is alike impossible for this element to
be absent from consciousness, and for it to be present in
consciousness alone: either alternative involves unconsciousness—the one from the want of the substance; the other from
the want of the form. But the persistence of this element
under successive conditions, *necessitates* a sense of it as distinguished from the conditions, and independent of them. The
sense of a something that is conditioned in every thought, cannot be got rid of, because the something cannot be got rid of.
How then must the sense of this something be constituted?
Evidently by combining successive concepts deprived of their
limits and conditions. We form this indefinite thought, as we
form many of our definite thoughts, by the coalescence of a
series of thoughts. Let me illustrate this: A large complex
object, having attributes too numerous to be represented at
once, is yet tolerably well conceived by the union of several rep-

resentations, each standing for part of its attributes. On thinking of a piano, there first rises in imagination its visual appearance, to which are instantly added (though by separate mental
acts) the ideas of its remote side and of its solid substance. A
complete conception, however, involves the strings, the ham-
mers, the dampers, the pedals ; and while successively adding
these to the conception, the attributes first thought of lapse more
or less completely out of consciousness. Nevertheless, the
whole group constitutes a representation of the piano. Now as
in this case we form a definite concept of a special existence, by
imposing limits and conditions in successive acts ; so, in the con-
verse case, by taking away the limits and conditions in successive acts, we form an indefinite notion of general existence. By
fusing a series of states of consciousness, in each of which, as it
arises, the limitations and conditions are abolished, there is produced a consciousness of something unconditioned. To speak
more rigorously :—this consciousness is not the abstract of any
one group of thoughts, ideas, or conceptions ; but it is the
abstract of *all* thoughts, ideas, or conceptions. That which is
common to them all, and cannot be got rid of, is what we predicate by the word existence. Dissociated as this becomes from
each of its modes by the perpetual change of those modes, it
remains as an indefinite consciousness of something constant
under all modes—of being apart from its appearances. The
distinction we feel between special and general existence, is the
distinction between that which is changeable in us, and that
which is unchangeable. The contrast between the Absolute and
the Relative in our minds, is really the contrast between that
mental element which exists absolutely, and those which exist
relatively.

"By its very nature, therefore, this ultimate mental element is
at once necessarily indefinite and necessarily indestructible.

Our consciousness of the unconditioned being literally the unconditioned consciousness, or raw material of thought to which in thinking we give definite forms, it follows that an ever-present sense of real existence is the very basis of our intelligence. As we can in successive mental acts get rid of all particular conditions and replace them by others, but cannot get rid of that undifferentiated substance of consciousness which is conditioned anew in every thought; there ever remains with us a sense of that which exists persistently and independently of conditions. At the same time that by the laws of thought we are rigorously prevented from forming a conception of absolute existence; we are by the laws of thought equally prevented from ridding ourselves of the consciousness of absolute existence : this consciousness being, as we here see, the obverse of our self-consciousness. And since the only possible measure of relative validity among our beliefs, is the degree of their persistence in opposition to the efforts made to change them, it follows that this which persists at all times, under all circumstances, and cannot cease until consciousness ceases, has the highest validity of any.

" To sum up this somewhat too elaborate argument :—We have seen how in the very assertion that all our knowledge, properly so called, is Relative, there is involved the assertion that there exists a Non-relative. We have seen how, in each step of the argument by which this doctrine is established, the same assumption is made. We have seen how, from the very necessity of thinking in relations, it follows that the Relative is itself inconceivable, except as related to a real Non-relative. We have seen that unless a real Non-relative or Absolute be postulated, the Relative itself becomes absolute ; and so brings the argument to a contradiction. And on contemplating the process of thought, we have equally seen how impossible it is to

get rid of the consciousness of an actuality lying behind appearances ; and how, from this impossibility, results our indestructible belief in that actuality."[1]

Such an extract as this is very tempting to the critic, but I
shall try not to be drawn into criticisms which do not immediately concern my purpose in quoting.   The points which chiefly
interest me are Mr. Spencer's evident confusion of sameness in
sense seventh with sameness in sense first, and of sameness in
sense second with sameness in sense first.   I shall begin with the
first confusion.

Every careful reader of the extract given above must see that
the Absolute with which Mr. Spencer's argument is concerned is
an Absolute in consciousness.   It is "an indefinite consciousness," "raw material of consciousness," an "indefinite
thought," an "abstract of *all* thoughts, ideas, or conceptions."
It is the element of existence which is common to all these
thoughts, ideas, or conceptions.   If there could be any doubt as
to the nature of this Absolute in which the argument results, it
should be set at rest by the very emphatic statement that "our
consciousness of the unconditioned" is "literally the unconditioned consciousness, or raw material of thought to which in
thinking we give definite forms."   It is this "undifferentiated
substance of consciousness which is conditional anew in every
thought" that remains with us as an Absolute through all
forms of the conditioned.

Now this Absolute, the element of existence which accom-
panies all other elements in consciousness, is the only one with
which the argument has at all concerned itself, and yet this is
evidently not the Absolute in which the author is chiefly interested.   There can be no good reason for calling this Absolute
either Unknowable, Incomprehensible, or Inscrutable.   It is not

---

[1] "First Principles," Part 1, Chap. IV, § 26, N. Y., 1888, pp. 93-97.

a "Power" for it is simply the element of existence, nor is it a "Reality," for the "abstract of *all* thoughts, ideas, or conceptions" must be common to the unreal or imaginary as well as to the real. It is (mental) existence pure and simple. If the argument be good, this element is known completely and just as it is; indefinitely, it is true, but then it is indefinite, and if known definitely would not be known as it is. There is nothing farther about it to know. It is in no sense Unknowable. If the objection be to the use of the word "know" where the knowledge is indefinite, we should invent some word to apply to an indefinite consciousness; but such consciousness, if denied to be knowledge, should not be classed with ignorance. Moreover, as knowledge is of all degrees of definiteness, we should need a series of words to express the gradations. The series would be a long one.

But the Absolute which interests Mr. Spencer, and which throws that halo of the mysterious about his philosophy, is a something distinct from the Absolute in consciousness, and not known as it is. It is by no means that which is common to "impressions" made upon us, but the something assumed to make these impressions. It is "under," "apart from," and "behind" appearances and modes—which an Absolute, which is simply that which is common to appearances and modes, cannot be. Phenomena (the things immediately known) are only "a manifestation of some Power by which we are acted upon,"[1] and this Absolute cannot take its place among phenomena, as the former must. The two Absolutes are, indeed, quite distinct things: one of them, the one in consciousness, has been shown to exist ; no argument is forthcoming to prove the existence of the other. Manifestly it is not immediately known, for then it would be a phenomenon, however indefinite. Upon what ground is it inferred? It is the old problem of Descartes and Locke.

[1] "First Principles." Chap. V, § 27, p. 99.

This problem Mr. Spencer solves in the same way as they, by assuming the "external" object to be given immediately; but there is this important difference, that whereas Descartes and Locke fall into the error from inadvertence, the author of the "First Principles" and the "Principles of Psychology" embraces it deliberately. The two earlier writers were sometimes able to recognize as two things a something in consciousness and an assumed something without. They confused them only now and then. Mr. Spencer has been unable to distinguish them with clearness at any time, and he elevates the confusion into a principle.

"The postulate with which metaphysical reasoning sets out, is that we are primarily conscious only of our sensations—that we certainly know we have these, and that if there be anything beyond these serving as cause for them, it can be known only by inference from them.

"I shall give much surprise to the metaphysical reader if I call in question this postulate; and the surprise will rise into astonishment if I distinctly deny it. Yet I must do this. Limiting the proposition to those epi-peripheral feelings produced in us by external objects (for these are alone in question) I see no alternative but to affirm that the thing primarily known, is not that a sensation has been experienced, but that there exists an outer object."[1]

"The question here is—What does consciousness directly testify? And the direct testimony of consciousness is, that Time and Space are not within but without the mind; and so absolutely independent of it that they cannot be conceived to become non-existent even were the mind to become non-existent."[2]

The moral of the first bit quoted would seem to be, unless we make the word "primarily" refer only to order in time, that one

---

[1] "Principles of Psychology," Part VII, Chap. VI. N. Y., 1883, Vol. II, p. 369.

[2] "First Principles," Part I, Chap. III, § 15. ed. cit. p. 49.

knows immediately what is beyond consciousness and mediately what is in it—a use of words satisfactory, I should think, to no one but Mr. Spencer. If, by "primarily" be meant "previously," and the two classes of being are known in just the same way, why distinguish between the classes? Moreover, in this case a thing would not be known "through" appearances, but before them. Upon the other supposition, to be sure, appearances would be known "through" it—a mode of speaking not in harmony with the language of the "First Principles." It seems a choice between Scylla and Charybdis.

The second extract makes consciousness "directly testify" not only to what is beyond its pale, but, putting on the spirit of prophecy, even to what does not belong to the present, but to a possible future. When we speak of consciousness as testifying to a sensation, we mean simply that the sensation is in consciousness. The word cannot be used in this sense in speaking of what is beyond consciousness. In what sense is it used? It would seem to mean, if it mean anything, that consciousness gives one the right to infer a something beyond—a right which thoughtful men believe should be established by proof. This proof, one cannot, of course, expect from a man who makes the thing beyond consciousness the thing "primarily" known. It would be more consistent in him to attempt a proof that there is something in consciousness.

This complete confusion in Mr. Spencer's mind of things in consciousness and things without, will explain why he keeps talking of his two Absolutes as if there were only one, as if this one were the one of which we are conscious, and yet as if this one were beyond consciousness. His pages swarm with illustrations which I might give. I shall give only the following: "Thus the consciousness of an Inscrutable Power manifested to us through all phenomena, has been growing ever clearer; and must eventually be freed from its imperfections."[1] If Mr. Spencer ever comes to a consciousness that sameness in sense seventh is not sameness in sense first, he will find work before him in remodeling his doctrine.

The second confusion upon which I wish to comment comes to the surface in a sentence occurring near the end of the lengthy extract quoted at the outset : "And since the only possible measure of relative validity among our beliefs, is the degree of their persistence in opposition to the efforts made to change them, it follows that this which persists at all times, under all circumstances, and cannot cease until consciousness ceases, has the highest validity of any."

Now that which, it has been argued, persists at all times and under all circumstances, is the "raw material of thought," the element of existence which is the "abstract of *all* thoughts, ideas, or conceptions." It is merely that which they have in common, and can include none of those elements in which they differ. If, however, persistence mean anything, it means persistence in time. That which exists at this time and that which exists at that are not one, strictly speaking, but two. That is, they are not the same in sense first, but in some looser sense which will admit of duality. If, then, we are dealing with the Absolute, existence pure and simple, and are abstracting from all differences which may mark out *this* existence from *that*, we must abstract from temporal distinctions too. If we do this, we can no longer speak of the Absolute as persisting. If we do not do this, something may persist, but it is no Absolute. Mental elements otherwise similar, but distinguished from each other by temporal differences are the same in sense second, not in sense first. The existence of which I am conscious to-day and the existence of which I was conscious yesterday are not the same existence in

[1] " First Principles," Part I, Chap. V, § 31, p. 108.

any sense save this. Yesterday's existence does not persist to-day; it is replaced by another. Mr. Spencer has evidently fallen into the error of those schoolmen who endeavored to abstract the element which several things have in common, but created unnecessary difficulties by making an incomplete abstraction and treating it as though it were complete. Other defects of this fallacious argument to prove our belief in the Absolute valid, I will not here discuss.

Sec. 35. I next take a few passages which will illustrate the confusion of samenesses first and seventh, from Dr. James Mc-Cosh's late work on "First and Fundamental Truths." They are selected from the chapter on "Our Intuition of Body by the Senses."[1]

"We are following the plainest dictates of consciousness, we avoid a thousand difficulties, and we get a solid ground on which to rest and to build, when we maintain that the mind in its first exercises acquires knowledge; not, indeed, scientific or arranged, not of qualities of objects and classes of objects, but still knowledge—the knowledge of things presenting themselves, and as they present themselves; which knowledge, individual and concrete, is the foundation of all other knowledge, abstract, general and deductive. In particular, the mind is so constituted as to attain a knowledge of body or of material objects. It may be difficult to ascertain the exact point or surface at which the mind and body come together and influence each other, in particular, how far into the body (Descartes without proof thought to be in the pineal gland), but it is certain that when they do meet mind knows body as having its essential properties of extension and resisting energy. It is through the bodily organism that the intelligence of man attains its knowledge of all material objects beyond. This is true of the infant mind; it is true also of the

[1] Part II, Book I, Chap. II.

mature mind. We may assert something more than this regarding the organism. It is not only the medium through which we know all bodily objects beyond itself; it is itself an object primarily known; nay, I am inclined to think that, along with the objects immediately affecting it, it is the only object originally known. Intuitively man seems to know nothing beyond his own organism, and objects directly affecting it; in all further knowledge there is a process of inference proceeding on a gathered experience. This theory seems to me to explain all the facts, and it delivers us from many perplexities."[1]

"In our primitive cognition of body there is involved a knowledge of Outness or Externality. We know the object perceived, be it the organism or the object affecting the organism, as not in the mind, but as out of the mind. In regard to some of the objects perceived by us, we may be in doubt as to whether they are in the organism or beyond it, but we are always sure that they are extra-mental."[2]

"We know the Objects as Affecting Us. I have already said that we know them as independent of us. This is an important truth. But it is equally true and equally important that these objects are made known to us as somehow having an influence on us. The organic object is capable of affecting our minds, and the extra-organic object affects the organism which affects the mind. Upon this cognition are founded certain judgments as to the relations of the objects known to the knowing mind."[3]

"But it will be vehemently urged that it is most preposterous to assert that we know all this by the senses. Upon this I remark that the phrase *by the senses* is ambiguous. If by senses he meant the mere bodily organism—the eye, the ears, the nerves and the brain—I affirm that we know, and can know, nothing by this bodily part, which is a mere organ or instru-

[1] N. Y., 1889, pp. 62-63.   [2] Pp. 68-69.   [3] P. 70.

ment; that so far from knowing potency or extension, we do not know even color, or taste, or smell. But if by the senses he meant the mind exercised in sense-perception, summoned into activity by the organism, and contemplating cognitively the external world, then I maintain that we do know, and this intuitively, external objects as influencing us ; that is, exercising powers in reference to us. I ask those who would doubt of this doctrine of what it is that they suppose the mind to be cognizant in sense-perception. If they say a mere sensation or impression in the mind, I reply that this is not consistent with the revelation of consciousness, which announces plainly that what we know is something extra-mental. If they say, with Kant, a mere phenomenon in the sense of appearance, then I reply that this, too, is inconsistent with consciousness, which declares that we know the thing."[1]

The statements contained in these extracts are plainly in a state of civil war, and might be left, without foreign aid, to complete their own destruction. I shall first let them criticize each other.

(1) It is asserted that it may be difficult to ascertain the exact point or surface at which the mind and body come together and influence each other—in particular how far into the body—but that it is certain that *when they do meet* mind knows body as having its essential properties of extension and resisting energy.

This knowledge is said to arise *when they meet*, be it marked, and not before.

(2) It is also asserted that it is *through the body* that the mind attains its knowledge of *all* material objects beyond.

This makes our knowledge of objects beyond the body mediate and not immediate. Why are objects beyond the body regarded as mediately known? No reason is suggested except that they are not themselves in contact with the mind, but only in contact with that which is in contact with the mind. It is then presumable that *any parts of the bodily organism which never themselves meet the mind (if there are any such) are not known immediately*, but only through the parts which do meet the mind. That is, they are known mediately, too. That there are, or at least may be, such parts, is directly inferrible from the statement that we do not know "how far into the body" mind and body come together.

(3) It is stated that the body is an object "primarily" known. It is regarded by the author as probable that, along with the objects immediately affecting it, it is the only object "originally" known. He thinks that man knows "intuitively" nothing beyond his own organism and objects directly affecting it.

But what is meant by the words "primarily," "originally," "intuitively"? If things not in direct contact with mind are not known immediately but through something else, and if the point or surface at which mind and body meet is at some uncertain distance from the surface of the body, surely the only material thing immediately known is that portion of the body in contact with mind, and not the whole body with the objects directly affecting it. Knowledge of these mediate objects must be due to a process of inference from what is directly experienced. *Things known "primarily," "originally" and "intuitively" are then known mediately and inferentially*—even in some cases so imperfectly known that it is not known what and where they are, whether in or beyond the body.

(4) The doctrine that we are conscious in sense-perception of a mere sensation or impression in the mind is answered by the statement that this is not consistent with the revelation of consciousness, which announces plainly that what we know is

something extra-mental. Kant's phenomenalism is met by the claim that consciousness declares that we know the thing.

A thing known mediately, however, cannot be more certainly known than the thing known immediately, and from which its existence is inferred. *The immediate revelation of consciousness cannot do more than give us a knowledge of the point or surface at which mind and body meet.* It is only here that mind can directly know body "as having its essential properties of extension and resisting energy." *But so far from consciousness testifying to the extension and resistance of this part of the body, it does not, as Dr. McCosh admits, testify to this part of the body at all.* If it reveal nothing as to what it knows immediately, what can its statement as to what it knows mediately be worth? And if consciousness testifies that it knows immediately what Dr. McCosh has maintained to be mediately known, he must hold that its revelation is false and delusive. It certainly seems to me that my consciousness reveals the ink-stand before me as it does not reveal the part of my body with which the mind has "come together," since it does not even reveal whether this part be a point or a surface. If my knowledge of the ink-stand must rest upon my knowledge of this, and can have no greater certainty, my faith in the ink-stand must go. A tower cannot be more firm than its foundation.

So much for the consistency of the extracts themselves. I now turn to a criticism on a different basis. The difficulties connected with this inconsistent doctrine naturally arise out of the standpoint occupied by the author. He accepts as final, and as justifiable in metaphysics, the convenient psychological assumption that the group of sensations gained from an object is a something distinct from the object itself; that the object may be external to the organism, but that the mind, with its sensations, is, or may be treated as if it were, somewhere within the organism; that the sensations are gained from real things, but are not themselves real things, so that a world of sensations—things being abstracted—must be an unreal and phantom world.

Now, the man who has thus distinguished between things and sensations, if he regard the sensations as our only immediate representatives of the things, will find it difficult, without making an evidently gratuitous assumption somewhere, to prove his right to reach things at all. Dr. McCosh sees this difficulty, and so he assumes that consciousness reveals both sensations and things. He allows us "perceptions mingled with sensations."[1] Where are these mingled perceptions and sensations? In the mind. Where is the mind? In the body. In what body? The body perceived. Is this body perceived itself in the mind and mingled with sensations? No. It is then distinct from the mental percept—the perception of it is somewhere in it, but is not it. How do we know, then, that there is a body? We infer it from the percept; consciousness (the percept) "reveals" it. On what principle is it inferred? The question is a just one if the knowledge be not immediate. Our author does not even see that there is a question. The fact is that this doctrine seems to avoid the difficulties of a representative perception only while it is allowed to remain loose and vague. If things are not to be known representatively, they must either be themselves in consciousness—*and then they are not extra-mental*—or they must be directly known in some other way than as in consciousness, *and then consciousness does not reveal them and cannot be appealed to.* An appeal to consciousness, unless the thing itself is in consciousness, is fatal.

But this discrimination between sensations and the thing causing the sensations, and the assumption that consciousness

---

[1] Chap. III, p. 75.

testifies to the two classes of things, does not seem to be borne
out by the facts. Consciousness does not testify to the two
classes. The common man thinks that he knows directly the
things that he sees and feels, and the distinction between these
things and his ideas of the things, or his sensations gathered
from the things, arises only upon reflection and after a comparison of his experiences with those of other men. He sees the
ink-stand in front of another man's body. He discovers that
the other man sees the ink-stand—that is, has an experience like
his own. He finds, after investigation, that this other man does
not have the experience until after some influence has been conducted by the nerves to the brain. He accordingly concludes
that the mind of this other man, and all that it *immediately*
knows, is situated somewhere in the brain. He thus distinguishes between the ink-stand and the representative of the
ink-stand in the mind of the other man. This is precisely what
Dr. McCosh has done, though he has preferred to use the word
perception instead of sensation or impression. Having gone as
far as this, the man in question reflects, if he be consistent, that
his own case must be essentially similar to that of the man he
is considering, and concludes that he, too, sees only (immediately, at least) some representative of the ink-stand, and not the
thing itself. Dr. McCosh does not conclude this, because he is
not consistent. But an ink-stand, a tree, a house, in the brain,
cannot be very much like a real ink-stand, tree or house. Then
one does not see things as they are, but is condemned to a
phantom world. Having gone thus far, our common man is
appalled at his own conclusions, as well he may be.

He may, however, be readily reassured, if one will point out
to him the error in his argument. The whole argument began
by assuming that he has evidence that some object is in front of
his body and in front of the body of another man ; that he has

a body and so has the other man. If this knowledge be immediate, of course it may furnish the basis of an argument ; but if
it be not immediate, one has no right to begin with it, but should
go back to what is immediate. Let us assume that it is immediate. What I am then conscious of is my own body, the other
man's body and the object in relation to them. Upon this basis
I argue to some representative of the object I immediately see,
and I connect it with the man's brain. Does the man now see
two objects or only one ? If only one, which one ? The one I
refer to his brain, or the one I see? Does the one he sees
seem to him to be in his brain? Probably he has not the least
notion that it is connected with that organ. Am I, then, in his
case? Do I also see only a copy of the object in my brain ?
And may this not be true, although I have no immediate knowledge of my brain and its relation to that object ? But—and this
is the important point—if all this be true, how about the position with which I started? My argument is based upon two
real bodies and a real object. I see that I was wholly in error
in supposing that I saw these and could reason from them.
Then the reasoning is not good. Then the conclusion is not
reliable, and it is not proved that I see immediately only an
image in, or in some sort of contact with, my brain. The fallacious character of the argument is plain enough ; where is the
flaw ? It lies in this :

I assume that I see the two bodies and the object immediately.
Consciousness seems to reveal them. After granting the man
opposite me a representative of that object I apply the same
reasoning to myself, forgetting that I assumed at the outset that
I see the real object. I can certainly not put the object I see in
my brain, for the brain in any way I can be conceived to know
it belongs to precisely the same class of things as this object,
and they are beside each other in consciousness. The represent-

ative the other man has is a representative of the object in my
consciousness, and not—at least, I have no evidence that it is—
a representative of a something else of which my object is also
a representative. And if the object of which I am immediately
conscious is extended and without my body (immediately perceived), I may assume that the object in his consciousness is also
extended and without the body in his consciousness. His rep.
resentative of my object is not in the head I see, for his head as
I see it is in my consciousness, if the object I see is, and any
object in his consciousness is the same with any corresponding
object in mine only in sense sixth—a sense of sameness which
I have explained at length in the earlier part of my work. This
reasoning is, it seems to me, clear enough and consistent enough,
and should be plain to any one who will take the trouble to follow it carefully. It lands one in no such difficulties and incon-
sistencies as result from the doctrine I have been criticizing.
Should it be said this is a form of Idealism, and at least abandons what is extra-mental, I answer, the name is a matter of
taste and of little significance ; what is important is that this
doctrine does not found its reasoning upon an assumption which
its conclusion declares to be false ; nor does it maintain that
what is immediately known is not extended, figured, external to
the body, as it seems to be, but something quite different and
dissimilar. It is in harmony with the revelation of consciousness. Should it still be objected that it makes no distinction
between things and the sensations or impressions which represent them, I answer, one can object to things being regarded as
complexes of sensations only as long as he separates sensations
and things, making the former unlike the things and relegating
them to a place (the brain) where the things are not, and to
exist in which they must be very bad copies of the things
indeed. The doctrine I advocate does not deny the things as
perceived at all ; it merely holds that consciousness does declare

for the things, and not for a set of representatives much unlike them and said to exist in a place in which we are not conscious of perceiving anything. It objects to seeing double through an incomplete reflection upon what consciousness reveals.

Now it is very evident that Dr. McCosh, in his anxiety to prove an extra-mental world, is actuated by a desire to retain real things. He is under the impression that, unless the extra-mental is known, our knowledge is confined to shadows and unrealities. He combats the Idealist, because he supposes him to deny the body of which we are conscious; whereas, all that the Idealist is denying (if he be consistent with his principles) is the hypothetical representative of the body, assumed to exist within the body, and to which consciousness does not testify. It is this that is the unreality. The body to which the Idealist holds is the very body to which Dr. McCosh thinks consciousness testifies; but this body is not beyond consciousness, nor in any proper sense of the words extra-mental. The above argument for the extra-mental is consequently due to a misconception—to the misconception that the body revealed by conscious-ness is the extra-mental body, and that the only body left to an Idealist is an unreal phantom of this body, and distinct from it. And it is the attempt to make this body revealed by conscious-ness both in mind and out of mind that has occasioned the difficulties and inconsequences of the reasoning I have quoted. This attempt is due to a confusion of sameness in sense seventh with sameness in sense first. My excuse for so minute a criticism of this plainly untenable position is that we have here a representative instance of an error quite common, and indeed characteristic of a certain stage of reflection.

SEC. 36. The last confusion of samenesses that I shall discuss lies at the bottom of the common opinion on the infinite divisibility of space, and causes the antinomies which arise from it. The position I shall criticize is well set forth in Professor W. K.

Clifford's popular lecture entitled "Of Boundaries in General."[1] From this I take a few passages which will suffice to illustrate his doctrine.

"Now the idea expressed by that word *continuous* is one of extreme importance ; it is the foundation of all exact science of things; and yet it is so very simple and elementary that it must have been almost the first clear idea that we got into our heads. It is only this : I cannot move this thing from one position to another, without making it go through an infinite number of intermediate positions. *Infinite ;* it is a dreadful word, I know, until you find out that you are familiar with the thing which it expresses. In this place it means that between any two positions there is some intermediate position; between that and either of the others, again, there is some other intermediate; and so on *without any end.* Infinite means without any end. If you went on with that work of counting forever, you would never get any further than the beginning of it. At last you would only have two positions very close together, but not the same ; and the whole process might be gone over again, beginning with those as many times as you like."

* * * * " When a point moves, it moves along some line; and you may say that it traces out or describes the line. To look at something definite, let us take the point where this boundary of red on paper is cut by the surface of water. I move all about together. Now you know that between any two positions of the point there is an infinite number of intermediate positions. Where are they all ? Why, clearly, in the line along which the point moved. That line is the place where all such points are to be found."

* * * * "It seems a very natural thing to say that space is made up of points. I want you to examine very carefully

1 " Seeing and Thinking," London, Macmillan & Co., 1879.

what this means, and how far it is true. And let us first take the simplest case, and consider whether we may safely say that a line is made up of points. If you think of a very large number—say, a million—of points all in a row, the end ones being an inch apart; then this string of points is altogether a different thing from a line an inch long. For if you single out two points which are next one another, then there is no point of the series between them; but if you take two points on a line, however close together they may be, there is an infinite number of points between them. The two things are different *in kind*, not in degree."

* * * * "When a point moves along a line, we know that between any two positions of it there is an infinite number (in this new sense[1]) of intermediate positions. That is because the motion is continuous. Each of those positions is where the point was at some instant or other. Between the two end positions on the line, the point where the motion began and the point where it stopped, there is no point of the line which does not belong to that series. We have thus an infinite series of successive positions of a continuously moving point, and in that series are included all the points of a certain piece of line-room. May we say then that the line is made up of that infinite series of points?

"Yes; if we mean no more than that the series makes up the *points* of the line. But *no*, if we mean that the line is made up of those points in the same way that it is made up of a great many very small pieces of line. A point is not to be regarded as a *part* of a line, in any sense whatever. It is the boundary between two parts."

These extracts suffice, I think, to show what the common doctrine is, and to show also the unavoidable difficulties connected

---

[1] Professor Clifford has used the word *number* in two senses, a quantitative and a qualitative. By number in the latter sense he means simply *unlimited units.*

with it. These were clearly seen long ago. Motion, argues Zeno of Elea,[1] cannot begin, because a body in motion must pass through an infinite number of intermediate places before it can arrive at any other place. Achilles can never overtake the tortoise, for by the time that he has reached the place where it was, it has always moved a little beyond. If Professor Clifford could not move a thing from one position to another, without making it go though an infinite number of intermediate positions, if these positions must be gone through with successively, and if infinite really mean *without any end*, then the final member of the series could never have been reached, for the plain reason that there is no final member to an endless series. If the new position is reached without passing through every member of the series and leaving none farther to pass through, it is not reached by passing through an infinite number of intermediate positions. The difficulty here is a hopeless one; either the series has a final member, *and then it is not infinite;* or it has not, *and then one cannot come to the end.*

The attempt sometimes made to avoid this difficulty by calling upon a precisely similar one for aid is of not the least avail. The time of the motion, it is said, is divisible just as is the space over which the body moves; the spaces and the times then vary together, and as the spaces become very small the times become very small; infinitesimal spaces are passed over in infinitesimal times, and all these infinitesimals are included in the finite space and finite time of the motion. But if there be a difficulty in arriving at the end of an endless series of places or positions, there is surely no less a difficulty in reaching the end of an endless series of times. If the series of times to be successively exhausted be truly endless, then an end of the motion can never be reached. Quibbling over the size of the members of the

[1] Ueberweg, Hist. of Philos., Vol. I, § 20. N. Y., 1877, pp. 57-58.

series in the case of either space or time is useless. Whether things are big or little, if the supply of them is truly endless, one can never get to the end of the supply. The rapidity with which they are exhausted has nothing to do with the question, for an increase in rapidity has obviously no effect in facilitating an approach to what is assumed not to exist, a final term. It is, then, perfectly clear that, if, in order to move a body, I must come to the end of an endless series, I may reasonably conclude that I cannot move a body. Granting the assumption upon which it is based, Zeno's argument is unanswerable. It is not a question of an ordinary difficulty, a trifling evil; it is a question of an impossibility, a flat contradiction; to move an inch, to endure for a minute, one is to accomplish the feat of reaching the end of the endless. One thing is quite certain; no rival doctrine can present a greater difficulty.

It is possible that some one may wish to find a way out of this difficulty by distinguishing, as Clifford has done, between the *points* of the line and the *parts* of the line. But this distinction is of no service. All these points are declared to be on the line, and anything that passes over the whole line must exhaust them one by one until it arrives at the final point. By hypothesis, there is no final point to the series—the series is without any end. Unless, then, the line can be passed over without passing over the points, there would seem to be no help in turning to line pieces. Moreover, it appears reasonable to assume that there are as many parts to the line as there are points. For all these points are on the line, and no two of them are in precisely the same position on the line; they must consequently be on different parts of the line. If it be objected that, having no extension, they cannot properly be said to be *on* parts of the line, I answer that, even on this hypothesis, they must be *at* different parts of the line, in order to be distinguished from each other. The part of the line between any two of them is certainly not the same as the part between any other two. It follows that the number of parts of which the line is made up is at least as great as the number of points less one, if we refuse to say that the points are on the line; and is as great as the number of points, if we are willing to say that they are on the line. To move over the whole line, then, a point must come within one term of the end of an endless series, or it must pass over an endless number of small pieces of line until it comes to the very end. Does this seem a sensible doctrine?

The rival doctrine, sometimes called the Berkeleyan, contains no such difficulties, and it makes evident that the difficulties discussed above arise simply out of a confusion of samenesses, and are gratuitous. Its discussion demands that I call to mind a few distinctions already made.

One must bear in mind, in the first place, that a line immediately known, existing in consciousness, is the same with an "external" line corresponding to it, not in sense first, but in sense seventh. That is, they are two lines, not one, and in the interests of clearness they should be considered separately.

One should remember, in the second place, that a line in consciousness at one moment is not, in the strictest sense, the same with a line in consciousness at another moment. One may stand for the other and thus be the same with it in sense fifth; or the two may be regarded as both belonging to the one series of experiences, which, taken together, represent to us "an object," in which case they are the same in sense third. A thing the same with another thing in either of these senses is not necessarily much like it. It must only be able to serve as its representative.

Now I see a line about an inch long on the paper before me. It is a certain distance from my eyes. I shall concern myself for the present only with the line immediately perceived, which means for me so much sensation. If I move this line (which remains the same in sense third), nearer to me or farther away, I do not perceive the identical thing that I did before. My quantity of sensation is increased or diminished. If I keep the line at the same distance and change none of the conditions, the quantity of sensation remains presumably the same. The question arises, Is this line as actually experienced at this moment infinitely divisible or not? I can certainly conceive of it as divisible to some extent, for I see part out of part, and I can think of these parts as separated. But if this line were divided, the division would soon result in parts which could be seen, but which could not be seen to consist of part out of part. Were these apparently non-extended parts (they would remain the same in sense third), approached to the eyes, they, too, would be seen to consist of part out of part, but then I should simply have substituted for the apparently non-extended a representative which was extended. This would not prove that what was before in consciousness was extended and could be divided. Consciousness certainly seems to testify that any particular line in consciousness is composed of a limited number of indivisible parts, and when one adds to this reflection the consideration that a point moving over a given line does not appear to have an endless task before it, but soon arrives at the final term, one is irresistibly impelled to the conclusion that the parts of the line are not infinite, but that the division results in the indivisible, the simple element of sensation, which, joined with other such elements, makes an extended object, but which taken alone is not extended at all. The whole difficulty lies in keeping to the line and the parts with which one started. It is so easy to pass from sameness in sense first to sameness in sense third or sense fifth; it is so natural to bring an object which is, as we say, imperfectly seen, closer to the eye and thus substitute for what was seen before a new experience connected with it in the order of nature, confident that any system of relations derived from the latter may safely be carried over to all possible experiences connected with the former ; one does this so instinctively that a man may very readily suppose that he is still busied about the apparently non-extended element with which he started, when he is in reality dividing and sub-dividing its representative, which is evidently extended. But the question is not whether, when one has divided a line until the parts cannot be seen to consist of parts, one may substitute for these parts what evidently does consist of parts, and go on dividing that. The question is, whether an apparently non-extended element of a line in consciousness is divisible or not. Any argument from the possibility of dividing its substitutes evidently has nothing to do with this point.

It is plain that this doctrine, which makes any particular finite line in consciousness to consist of a limited number of simple parts, is not open to the objection that it necessitates the absurdity of exhausting an endless series. Moving along such a line, Achilles could overtake the tortoise, for the successively diminishing distances between them do not constitute an endless series The descending series results after a limited number of terms in the simple, and the series is broken, for the simple does not consist of parts. In this there is at least no contradiction. It remains to see what other objections may lie against it.

It may be argued, first, as it often is argued, that it is impossible to conceive of any part of a line as not itself extended and having parts. It may be admitted that the small parts arrived at do not *seem* to have part out of part ; that these sub-parts are not observed in them, but still it is said that one who thinks about them cannot but think of them as really having such parts. I ask one who puts forward this objection to look into his own mind and see whether he does not mean by "thinking about them," bringing them in imagination nearer to the eye, or by some means substituting for them what can be seen to have part out of part. That one can do this no one would think of denying, but, as I have said, this does not prove the original parts to be extended.

It may be objected again that extension can never be built up out of the non-extended—that if one element of a given kind has, taken alone, no extension at all, two or more such elements together cannot have any extension either. I answer that a straight line has no angularity at all, and yet two straight lines may obviously make an angle ; that one man is not in the least a crowd, but that one hundred men may be ; that no single tree is a forest, but that many trees together do make a forest ; that a uniform expanse of color is in no sense a variegated surface, but that several such together do make a variegated surface. It may be that extension is simply the name we give to several simple sense-elements of a particular kind taken together. One cannot say off-hand that it is not.

Should one object, finally, that, if a given line in conscious-ness be composed of a limited number of indivisible elements of sensation, consciousness ought to distinguish these single elements and testify as to their number ; I answer that what is in consciousness is not necessarily in a clear analytical conscious-ness, nor well distinguished from other elements. For example, I am at present conscious of a stream of sensations which I connect with the hand that holds my pen. The single elements in this complex I cannot distinguish from each other, nor can I give their number. It does not follow that I am to assume the number to be infinite. Much less should I be impelled to make this assumption, if it necessitated my accepting as true what I see to be flatly contradictory, as in the case under discussion. It was because of this vagueness and lack of discrimination in the testimony of consciousness that I said, some distance back, that consciousness *seems* to testify that any finite line in it is composed of simple parts. If the testimony were quite clear, the matter would be settled at once. As it is not quite clear, the matter has to be settled on a deductive basis. The most reasonable solution appears to be the Berkeleyan.

So much for the line immediately perceived, the line in consciousness. What shall we say to one who is willing to admit that this line is not infinitely divisible, but is composed of simple sense-elements; and yet who maintains that there exists an "external" line corresponding to it, which is not immediately perceived, and is infinitely divisible? We may begin by suggesting to him that an "external" point moving over this "external" line must perform the wholly impossible feat to which Clifford condemns a point moving over a line; and we may farther suggest that, if the "external" world be an intelligible world at all, a contradiction may be as much out of place in it as anywhere else. And if the existence of this world be problematic, a thing not self-evident, it seems quite reasonable to demand very good proof indeed of the existence of that which contains in its very conception such excellent reasons for believing in its non-existence. This proof, the student of the history of speculation will testify, has not as yet been forthcoming.

SEC. 37. With this I close my analysis of samenesses, and of confusions which have resulted in needless embarrassments and gratuitous difficulties. More instances of the latter could be given, of course. The reader will be able to furnish, I presume, many like them. Those which I have given seem to me quite sufficient to prove the need of much greater care and exactitude than one commonly finds in metaphysical reasonings. Loose reasoning is bad reasoning, and leads to bad results. Its one virtue is that it does not require much mental application on the part of either author or reader. On the other hand, the attempt to be cautious and exact, to distinguish between things easily confounded, and to keep strictly to the thing in dispute through a long discussion, these things are wearisome to all concerned. Although I am quite conscious of this fact, I have tried to do these things : with what result, my fellow-analysts must judge. I feel reasonably sure that I have succeeded in being wearisome, and for this I make due apology.

CONTENTS.

PART I.

THE KINDS OF SAMENESS.

PART II.

HISTORICAL AND CRITICAL.